KENWOOD

CREATE MORE

Published for Kenwood Ltd.
Edition 2013

Design: Pepper Creative
Recipe Development: Nicholas Ghirlando
Photography: Philip Webb
Food Stylist: Nicholas Ghirlando

Whilst every care has been taken in compiling
this book the publishers cannot accept
responsibility for any errors, inadvertent or not,
that may be found or may occur at some time
in the future, owing to changes in legislation
or for any other reason.

A CIP catalogue record for this book is available
from the British library.

ISBN 978-1-907367-29-8

CONTENTS

INTRODUCTION

This recipe book has been written for the Kenwood Chef and contains over 65 recipes to illustrate its many uses, covering a variety of baking, soups, drinks and dinner party recipes to inspire you to create more with your machine. Also offering a wide selection of attachments so that you can build and tailor your machine to your needs.

The first chapter is all about baking, the fundamentals of a Kenwood Chef. By the end of this chapter you will be able to master breads, cakes, pastries and much more. If you are feeling experimental or hosting a party why not try a dish from the Entertaining section and impress your guests, or try a heart warming soup or an iced cocktail within the soups and drinks section.

With a Kenwood Chef you truly can create more, get inspired visit www.kenwoodworld.com

THE AUTHOR

Nico Ghirlando is a versatile food writer and stylist who has created over 170 recipes for the Kenwood Chef. The following recipe book showcases Nico's favourite recipes, and he also completed the food and food styling for the book.

I hope you enjoy the book and the machine as much as I have enjoyed coming up with these recipes.

Nico

NICO GHIRLANDO

COOKERY NOTES

Use medium eggs unless otherwise stated.

Place dishes in the middle of the oven unless otherwise stated.

OVEN CONVERSION CHART

DEGREES FAHRENHEIT	DEGREES CELSIUS	GAS MARK	DESCRIPTION
225	110	1/4	Very slow
250	120/130	1/2	Very slow
275	140	1	Slow
300	150	2	Slow
325	160/170	3	Moderate
350	180	4	Moderate
375	190	5	Moderately hot
400	200	6	Moderately hot
425	220	7	Hot
450	230	8	Hot
475	240	9	Very Hot

Cooking times may vary slightly depending on each individual oven so it is recommended to check your dish towards the end of the cooking time.

VOLUMES

When measuring liquid, cooking measurements are quite straightforward:

METRIC	IMPERIAL	US CUPS
250ml	8 fl oz	1 cup
180ml	6 fl oz	3/4 cup
150ml	5 fl oz	2/3 cup
120ml	4 fl oz	1/2 cup
75ml	2 1/2 fl oz	1/3 cup
60ml	2 fl oz	1/4 cup
30ml	1 fl oz	1/8 cup
15ml	1/2 fl oz	1 tablespoon

AMERICAN CUP CONVERSIONS

AMERICAN	IMPERIAL	METRIC
1 cup flour	5oz	150g
1 cup caster/ granulated sugar	8oz	225g
1 cup brown sugar	6oz	175g
1 cup butter/margarine/lard	8oz	225g
1 cup ground almonds	4oz	110g
1 cup golden syrup	12oz	350g
1 cup uncooked rice	7oz	200g
1 cup grated cheese	4oz	110g
1 stick butter	4oz	110g

SPOONS

1 tablespoon	1/16 cup	1 teaspoon	5ml
2 tablespoons	1/8 cup	2 teaspoons	10ml
4 tablespoons	1/4 cup	1 tablespoon	15ml
5 tablespoons	1/3 cup	2 tablespoons	30ml
8 tablespoons	1/2 cup	3 tablespoons	45ml
10 tablespoons	2/3 cup	4 tablespoons	60ml
12 tablespoons	3/4 cup	5 tablespoons	75ml
16 tablespoons	1 cup	6 tablespoons	90ml
		7 tablespoons	105ml

GUIDE TO SYMBOLS

Level of difficulty is represented by the chef's hat symbols:

EASY

MEDIUM

DIFFICULT

The bowl tool or attachment you need for each recipe is represented by the following symbols:

K beater

Dough hook

Whisk

Creaming beater

Folding tool

Blender

Food processor

Compact chopper/grinder

Continuous slicer/grater

Pasta roller

Frozen dessert maker

BOWL TOOLS AND BLENDER

KENWOOD KITCHEN MACHINES ARE DESIGNED TO BEAT, KNEAD AND WHISK INGREDIENTS IN AN OPEN BOWL MAKING COOKING QUICKER, EASIER AND MORE PLEASURABLE.

Every mixing function from cakes, biscuits, pastry, doughs, meringues, mousses and souffles can all be achieved with the bowl tools.

Not all packs have the creaming beater, folding tool or blender included from the beginning but these can be bought separately to help with all your mixing needs.

K BEATER
ALMOND BISCUITS
8

DOUGH HOOK
24 HOUR PIZZA DOUGH
9

WHISK
MERINGUES WITH STRAWBERRIES & CREAM
10

CREAMING BEATER
CHOCOLATE GANACHE
11

FOLDING TOOL
MADELEINES
12

BLENDER
MANGO LASSI
13

K BEATER

THE K BEATER IS LIKELY TO BE THE MOST FREQUENTLY USED TOOL, IDEAL FOR MAKING CAKES, BISCUITS, PASTRY, ICING, FILLINGS, ÉCLAIRS AND MASHED POTATO. THE SPECIALLY DESIGNED CENTRAL 'K' MOVES THROUGH THE MIXTURE, ENSURING ALL INGREDIENTS ARE INCORPORATED THOROUGHLY.

WHEN BEST TO USE:

CREAMED MIXTURES
Creaming together fat and sugar for either a cake mix or icing.

RUBBED-IN MIXTURES
Blending flour and fat to a crumb-like mix for plain cakes, scones and biscuits.

CRUMBING BISCUITS
Crush biscuits for making cheesecake bases and flan cases.

MASHING VEGETABLES
Pre-cook potato, swede or parsnips and mix with a little butter until mashed.

K BEATER RECIPE
ALMOND BISCUITS

SERVES	Makes 12 biscuits
PREP TIME	10 mins
COOKING TIME	12-15 mins
DIFFICULTY	☻
EQUIPMENT	Baking tray, baking paper, flat pan
TOOLS	

INGREDIENTS

12 whole almonds, skinless
150g unsalted butter
200g caster sugar
½ tsp baking powder
150g flour
150g ground almonds
1 egg, beaten
1 tsp almond extract

METHOD

➤ Heat the oven to 180°C and line a baking tray with baking paper.

➤ Toast the 12 whole almonds in a dry flat pan and set aside.

➤ Add the sugar and butter to the bowl, attach the K beater and mix on a high speed until pale and fluffy.

➤ Add the baking powder, flour and ground almonds and mix well on a medium speed for one minute, then add the egg and almond extract and beat well until fully incorporated.

➤ Drop tablespoon sized amounts of the mixture onto the baking tray, leaving a good space between each one, top each one with the toasted almonds.

➤ **Cook in the oven for 12-15** minutes until golden. Remove and cool on a wire rack.

DOUGH HOOK

THE DOUGH HOOK TAKES THE HARD WORK OUT OF
KNEADING DOUGH. IT IS IDEAL FOR CREATING BREADS,
ROLLS, BUNS, PIZZA DOUGH AND SWEET DOUGH.

WHEN BEST TO USE:

BREADS/ROLLS/SWEET BREAD
Mixes and kneads flour, water and yeast.

PIZZA DOUGH
Mixes and kneads flour, water, yeast and oil.

DOUGH HOOK
RECIPE 24 HOUR
PIZZA DOUGH

SERVES	4
PREP TIME	5 mins, plus 24 hours for proving and rising
DIFFICULTY	●
EQUIPMENT	Rolling pin
TOOLS	

INGREDIENTS
500g strong white flour, type '00'
7g easy action dried yeast
1 tbsp sugar
100ml lukewarm water
1 tbsp salt
30ml olive oil

METHOD

▸ Attach the dough hook.

▸ Pour in the flour, yeast and sugar.
Turn the machine to a slow speed and
slowly add the water. Knead well for a
few minutes then add the salt.

▸ Turn the speed up to medium, add
the oil and knead for ten minutes.

▸ Remove the dough and place in a
large bowl, cover with a damp cloth
and leave to rise for two hours.

▸ Put the dough back into the Kitchen
Machine bowl and knock the air out,
leave to rise for a further two hours,
then cover with oiled clear film and put
in the fridge for up to 20 hours.

▸ Remove the dough from the fridge
and divide into four, roll each one
out thinly.

▸ Top with tomato purée, cheese and
toppings of your choice and **bake in a
very hot oven straight on the shelf for
8 to 10 minutes.**

WHISK

THE WHISK IS PERFECT FOR CREATING FOAMY
WHIPPED MIXTURES, IDEAL FOR EGGS, CREAM,
BATTERS, FATLESS SPONGES, MERINGUES,
CHEESECAKES, MOUSSES AND SOUFFLÉS. THE
BALLOON SHAPE OF THE WHISK MAXIMISES AERATION
FOR THE BEST POSSIBLE VOLUME AND TEXTURE

WHEN BEST TO USE:

EGG WHITES
Whisk eggs on a high speed for meringue, pavlova
and soufles.

BATTERS
Flour, milk and egg batters for pancakes, crépes and
Yorkshire pudding.

WHIPPING CREAM
Whisk cream on a medium speed to top pies, trifles, fill
sponges and profiteroles.

LIGHT SPONGES
Sponges without butter for swiss roll, roulade and
Genoese sponge.

WHIPPED DESSERTS
Egg yolks and fruit purees for mousses, cream and egg
whites for soufflés.

WHISK RECIPE
MERINGUES WITH STRAWBERRIES AND CREAM

SERVES	4
PREP TIME	15 minutes
COOKING TIME	45 minutes plus cooling
DIFFICULTY	⚙⚙
EQUIPMENT	Baking tray and baking paper
TOOLS	

INGREDIENTS
4 egg whites
200g icing sugar
1 punnet of strawberries, hulled
and quartered
Double cream, to serve

METHOD

‣ Heat the oven to 150°C. Line a
baking tray with baking paper.

‣ Attach the whisk and mixing bowl,
making sure they are spotlessly clean
and free of any grease.

‣ Add the egg whites and whisk on a
high speed for 3-4 minutes until you
have stiff peaks.

‣ Add the sugar a tablespoon at a time
until the mix is glossy.

‣ Spoon the meringue mixture onto
the lined baking tray into fist sized
portions, leaving a large gap between
each one.

‣ **Cook in the oven for 35-40
minutes.** Turn the heat off and leave
to cool in the oven.

‣ Serve with fresh strawberries and
cream.

CREAMING BEATER

THE CREAMING BEATER IS IDEAL FOR CREAMING
AND MIXING SOFT INGREDIENTS TOGETHER.
THE FLEXIBLE EDGES ACT AS A SPATULA PROVIDING
THE SMOOTHEST RESULTS.

WHEN BEST TO USE:

CAKE MIXES
Creaming together fat and sugar until pale and fluffy.

ICING
Mixing together icing sugar and butter to create icing
to top cakes.

CREAMING BEATER RECIPE
CHOCOLATE GANACHE

SERVES	Makes 300g
PREP TIME	10 mins
DIFFICULTY	☻
EQUIPMENT	Saucepan
TOOLS	

INGREDIENTS

100ml double cream
1 vanilla pod, split lengthways
200g 80% cocoa dark chocolate

METHOD

▶ Bring the cream and vanilla to just
below the boil in a saucepan.

▶ Attach the creaming beater.

▶ Break the chocolate into pieces
and put in the mixing bowl. Slowly
pour in the heated cream and turn the
machine to a medium speed and beat
until smooth.

▶ Scrape the chocolate mixture into
a separate bowl, cover and keep
somewhere cool until needed.

▶ Can be used for decorating a vanilla
sponge or cupcakes.

FOLDING TOOL

THE FOLDING TOOL IS PERFECT FOR COMBINING
HEAVIER INGREDIENTS INTO LIGHT AIRY INGREDIENTS
WHILST MAINTAINING THE AIR WITHIN THE MIXTURE.
IDEAL FOR MOUSSES, SOUFFLES, LIGHT SPONGES
AND MACAROONS.

WHEN BEST TO USE:

MAINTAINING AIR IN A MIXTURE

The folding tool allows a heavy ingredient to be
combined with a light airy mixture, lifting the food
up from around the sides of the bowl and dropping it
back in from above. This action maintains the texture
required to create light airy dishes.

FOLDING TOOL RECIPE
MADELEINES

SERVES	4 - 6
PREP TIME	10 minutes
COOKING TIME	10 - 12 minutes
DIFFICULTY	☻
EQUIPMENT	Madeleine tray, baking tray, baking paper
TOOLS	

INGREDIENTS

2 eggs
125g caster sugar
125g plain flour
125g melted butter
1 tsp baking powder
1 tbsp icing sugar

METHOD

➤ Heat the oven to 190°C and brush
a Madeleine tray with melted butter.
If you do not have a madeleine tray you
can use a flat baking tray lined with
baking paper.

➤ Add the eggs and sugar to the bowl,
attach the whisk and whisk together
until light and fluffy.

➤ Remove the whisk and attach
the folding tool, add the remaining
ingredients to the bowl and fold together
on a low speed until well combined
then set aside for ten minutes.

➤ Put a spoonful in each mould or
spoon tablespoons of the mixture onto
the lined baking tray, making sure you
leave space between each one.

➤ **Bake in the oven for 10-12 minutes**
until browning.

➤ Remove from the oven and leave to
cool on a wire rack, dust with a little
icing sugar and serve.

BLENDER

THE BLENDER ATTACHMENT IS IDEAL FOR MILKSHAKES, SMOOTHIES, COCKTAILS, SOUPS, SAUCES AND ICE CRUSHING. AVAILABLE IN A VARIETY OF STYLES AND MATERIALS INCLUDING THERMORESIST, GLASS AND PLASTIC.

WHEN BEST TO USE:

DRINKS
Blend fresh fruit, ice cream, yogurt, milk and fruit juice.

SOUPS
Blend cooked vegetables and stock.

SAUCES & DIPS
Able to blend small quantities for mayonnaise, salsa or hummus.

ICE CRUSHING
Crush ice, ideal for cocktails.

BLENDER RECIPE
MANGO LASSI

SERVES	4
PREP TIME	5 mins
DIFFICULTY	☻
TOOLS	

INGREDIENTS
2 ripe mangoes, peeled and stoned
200ml milk
200ml natural yogurt
Juice of 1 lime
1 tsp chilli powder (optional)

METHOD
➤ Pour all the ingredients apart from the chilli into the blender and blend on a high speed until smooth. Divide between four glasses and serve, sprinkled with the chilli powder.

QUICK START

THESE RECIPES ARE DESIGNED TO GET YOU STARTED STRAIGHT AWAY AND WILL HELP YOU GET TO KNOW THE KENWOOD CHEF A LITTLE BETTER. FROM A SIMPLE DOUGH TO A QUICK BISCUIT MIX THESE WILL PRODUCE GREAT RESULTS THAT YOU CAN ADAPT INTO MORE COMPLICATED RECIPES.

Once you have mastered the recipes in the quick start section you can work your way through the baking section and become a baking expert.

Eventually you will be able to produce bread, pastry, biscuits and layered cakes, and even adjust the recipes to your own personal tastes.

DOUGH

INGREDIENTS

7g easy action dried yeast
Pinch of sugar
500g strong bread flour
400ml water
Pinch of salt

STEP 1

In a bowl, add a little lukewarm water and sugar to the yeast and leave for ten minutes to activate.

STEP 2

Add the flour and salt to the bowl, pour in the yeast mix. Attach the dough hook and mix on a low speed for a minute.

STEP 3

Gradually add the water and turn the speed up to medium. Knead for ten minutes.

STEP 4

Cover the bowl with a damp cloth and leave to rise in a warm place for an hour, or until doubled in size.

STEP 5

Heat the oven to 180°C and grease a loaf tin. Add a few ice cubes to a tray and place in the bottom of the oven; this will help create a crisp crust.

STEP 6

Add the dough to the loaf tin and leave to rest for 15 minutes, then dust with flour.

STEP 7

Bake for 40 minutes, or until golden brown and the bottom sounds hollow when tapped. Leave to cool on a wire rack.

Why not try?...

RUSSIAN RYE TREACLE BREAD

See page 29

PASTRY

INGREDIENTS

225g flour
110g butter, chilled and cubed
50ml water
Salt

STEP 1

Add the flour and butter to the bowl, attach the K beater and mix on a medium speed until it resembles bread crumbs.

STEP 2

Turn the speed down and slowly add the water and salt. Mix until it comes together, away from the side of the bowl.

STEP 3

Remove the pastry from the bowl and wrap in clear film and leave to rest in the fridge for half an hour or in the freezer for 15 minutes.

The pastry is ready to use.

RECIPE IDEA
SAVOURY PASTRY

STEP 1

Roll out onto a lined baking tray and top with cherry tomatoes, sliced red onions, cooked asparagus and goats cheese.

STEP 2

Cook in a preheated oven at 180°C for 20 minutes, or until the pastry is golden and the cheese bubbling. Serve.

Why not try?...

CHICKEN, LEEK AND HAM PIE

See page 39

BATTER MIX

INGREDIENTS

150g flour
1 tsp salt
2 eggs
75ml olive oil
300ml milk

STEP 1

Add the flour and salt to the bowl and attach the K beater.

STEP 2

On a low speed gradually add the eggs, oil and milk. Turn the speed up to medium and mix until everything is incorporated.

STEP 3

Leave to rest for 10 minutes, ready to use.

RECIPE IDEA
PANCAKES

STEP 1

Heat some butter and oil in a large saute pan and add a ladleful of the batter to the centre turning the pan around so the mixture spreads evenly.

STEP 2

Cook for a minute or until bubbles appear and the edges start to crisp, then flip the pancake over and cook the other side.

STEP 3

Stack on greaseproof paper and serve with lemon and sugar.

SIMPLE SPONGE CAKE

INGREDIENTS

225g butter, softened
225g caster sugar
225g self raising flour
4 eggs
1 tbsp vanilla extract
1 tbsp icing sugar

STEP 1

Preheat the oven to 190°C, grease and line two 18cm cake tins.

STEP 2

Attach the creaming beater, add the butter and sugar and mix on a medium speed until creamy.

STEP 3

With the machine still running gradually add the flour until well incorporated, and then add the eggs a little at a time, mixing well between additions.

STEP 4

Pour in the vanilla extract and mix well.

STEP 5

Divide the mix between the cake tins and **bake for 25-30 minutes,** or until golden brown and a skewer inserted into the middle comes out clean.

STEP 6

Leave to cool.

RECIPE IDEA
BUTTER ICING AND JAM

INGREDIENTS

225g softened butter
500g icing sugar

STEP 1

Make a buttercream filling by mixing softened butter with icing sugar until smooth, leave to chill for 30 minutes.

STEP 2

Spread the butter icing onto one cake, and top with raspberry jam, place the other half of cake on top and dust with icing sugar. Serve.

BASIC MERINGUE

INGREDIENTS

4 egg whites
220g caster sugar

STEP 1

Attach the whisk, add the egg whites and whisk on a low speed until they start to lightly foam.

STEP 2

Turn the speed up to high and whisk for about 8 minutes, or until stiff peaks start to form.

STEP 3

Turn the speed down a little and add the sugar, a tablespoon at a time, until it is all incorporated and the meringue is glossy.

STEP 4

Use the meringue to top a pie.

Why not try?...

LEMON AND LIME PIE

See page **53**

COOKIES

INGREDIENTS

225g softened butter
150g golden caster sugar
1 egg yolk
1 tbsp vanilla extract or paste
280g plain flour

STEP 1

Heat the oven to 180°C and line a baking tray with baking paper.

STEP 2

Add the butter and sugar to the bowl, attach the K beater and mix on a medium speed until creamy.

Add the egg and vanilla and mix on a medium speed until combined.

STEP 3

With the machine on slow, add the flour a little at a time until fully combined.

STEP 4

Remove the dough from the bowl and roll out to 3 - 5mm thick.

STEP 5

Using a cookie cutter cut out biscuits and place them onto the baking tray, leaving a gap between each one so that they do not stick together.

STEP 6

Bake for 10-15 minutes, or until nicely golden. Leave to cool on a wire rack.

RECIPE IDEA
CHOC CHIP COOKIES

Sprinkle chocolate chips over the biscuits before you bake them.

THE WORLD OF BAKING IS SO RICH AND VARIED AND FULL OF SO MANY WONDERFUL DISHES THAT IT WAS DIFFICULT TO NARROW DOWN INTO ONE CHAPTER. ALL COUNTRIES HAVE VARIATIONS ON BREAD AND CAKES AND ALL PROVIDE MANY DIFFERENT TASTES AND TEXTURES.

Baking encompasses anything from bread and cake to pies, pastries and puddings and I've covered most of them here. This is where the Kenwood Chef really comes into its own and makes the whole process so much easier.

The dough hook saves so much time and effort with kneading and the trademark 'K Beater' is unrivalled. The process of baking can seem a little daunting at times, but it is a joy with the Kenwood Chef.

SOURDOUGH BREAD

THIS TAKES A LITTLE PREPARATION, IN AS
MUCH AS YOU NEED TO MAKE A 'STARTER'
DOUGH. HOWEVER, ONCE YOU'VE MADE IT,
YOU CAN KEEP IT ALIVE IN THE FRIDGE ALMOST
INDEFINITELY, AS LONG AS YOU FEED IT
REGULARLY. THE TASTE AND SATISFACTION
ARE WELL WORTH IT.

SERVES	Makes 2 loaves
PREP TIME	5 days for the starter, 25 minutes plus 3 hours rising time
COOKING TIME	30-35 minutes
TEMPERATURE	250°C / Gas 9
DIFFICULTY	●●
EQUIPMENT	Baking tray, baking paper and a shallow lined baking tray
TOOLS	

INGREDIENTS

For the starter:

125ml natural yoghurt
150ml buttermilk
400g rye flour
100g '00' strong flour
250ml water

For the loaves:

350ml water
550g strong white flour, plus a little extra for dusting
1 tsp salt
300g starter

METHOD

▸ Make the starter over five days by first
mixing together in a bowl the yoghurt, 100ml
buttermilk and stirring in 100g of the rye
flour. Cover and leave at room temperature
for 24 hours.

▸ The next day stir in 100g of the rye flour.
Cover and leave at room temperature for
48 hours.

▸ Remove about 100g of the starter mix. Add
200g more rye flour, 100ml of water and the
remaining 50ml buttermilk. Stir well, cover and
leave for a further 24 hours.

▸ The next day, add 100g of '00' flour and
150ml of water. Stir well, cover and leave for a
final 24 hours. It is then ready to use. Keep it in
the fridge and every 2-3 days discard one third
and replace with an equal amount of water and
rye flour and mix well. This way, you can keep
it alive and on hand almost indefinitely.

▸ To make the sourdough loaves add the
water, 500g strong white bread flour and salt
to the bowl. Pour in 300g of the starter, attach
the dough hook and knead well on a medium
speed for 10 minutes, until you have a strong,
smooth and elastic dough. Remove the bowl
and cover with a damp cloth and leave to rise
for 3 to 4 hours.

▸ Flour a work surface and remove the dough
from the bowl. Divide the dough into two,
knock the air out and shape into buns. Lightly
oil two bowls and place the dough into the
bowls, cover and leave for three hours.

▸ Heat the oven to 250°C and line a baking
tray with baking paper.

▸ Remove the dough from the bowls and place
onto a baking tray, give a good dusting of flour
and score a cross in the top of each loaf.

▸ Boil the kettle, pour some of the water into
a shallow baking tray and place in the bottom
of the oven (this creates steam to help make
a crust).

▸ **Bake the loaves in the oven for 35 minutes**
or until the bottom sounds hollow when
tapped. Leave to cool on a wire rack for about
an hour.

BAGUETTE

SERVES	Makes 3 baguettes
PREP TIME	25 minutes plus 7 hours rising time
COOKING TIME	20 minutes
TEMPERATURE	240°C / Gas 9
DIFFICULTY	😊 😊
EQUIPMENT	Baking sheet and shallow baking tray
TOOLS	

INGREDIENTS

2x 7g easy action dried yeast
1 tsp sugar
1kg plain flour plus a little extra for dusting
2 tsp salt
450-500ml water
Olive oil, for greasing

METHOD

▸ Preheat the oven to 240°C degrees.

▸ Attach the dough hook and add the yeast, sugar and a little warm water. Leave for 3-4 minutes until foaming, then add half the flour, 250ml of the water and salt.

▸ Knead for 5 minutes on a medium speed, then remove the bowl and cover with a damp cloth. Leave to rest in a warm place for 5 hours.

▸ Add the rest of the flour and water to the bowl and knead on a medium speed for ten minutes, until you have a very elastic dough.

▸ Oil the side of the bowl and cover the dough with a damp cloth. Leave overnight or for at least 2 hours.

▸ Knead the dough for a minute, remove from the bowl onto a floured surface and cut into three. Roll each into a baguette shape and with a sharp blade score each one four times diagonally and lightly dust with flour.

▸ Place on a baking sheet and leave for 15 minutes.

▸ Boil the kettle and pour some of the water into a shallow baking tray, place in the bottom of the oven (this creates steam to help make a crust).

▸ **Bake the baguettes for about 20 minutes**, until crisp and golden. Leave to cool on a wire rack and eat the same day.

CUMIN AND FENNEL CORN BREAD

CORN BREAD IS A DELICIOUS ALTERNATIVE TO TRADITIONAL LOAVES AND GIVES A SOFT, CRUMBLY DOUGH THAT IS GREAT FOR SOAKING UP SAUCES.

SERVES	4
PREP TIME	10 minutes
COOKING TIME	30 minutes
TEMPERATURE	200°C / Gas 6
DIFFICULTY	
EQUIPMENT	Loaf tin
TOOLS	

INGREDIENTS

1 tbsp fennel seeds
1 tbsp cumin seeds
1 tbsp ground fennel
1 tbsp ground cumin
250g plain flour
250g maize / polenta
1 tbsp baking powder
50ml water
1 tsp salt
2 eggs, beaten
250ml buttermilk
60g butter, melted
60g caster sugar

METHOD

▸ Heat the oven to 200°C and grease a loaf tin.

▸ Toast the fennel seeds and cumin seeds in a dry pan until fragrant - reserve.

▸ Add the flour, maize, baking powder, ground spices, water and salt to the bowl. Attach the dough hook.

▸ In a separate bowl mix together the eggs, buttermilk, melted butter and sugar. Add the mix to the bowl and knead on a high speed for about 10 seconds so that the mixture remains lumpy.

▸ Pour the mixture into the greased loaf tin, top with the fennel and cumin seeds and **bake for about half an hour** until the dough is firm and slightly springy. Leave to cool on a cooling rack and serve slightly warm.

WALNUT OIL
TIGER BREAD

A LOVELY SOFT LOAF WITH A CRUNCHY
TOPPING MADE WITH RICE FLOUR AND WALNUT
OIL. THIS GIVES IT THE TEXTURED PATTERN
THAT GIVES IT ITS NAME.

SERVES	4
PREP TIME	10 minutes plus 1 hour 30 minutes for rising and rest
COOKING TIME	25-30 minutes
TEMPERATURE	200°C / Gas 6
DIFFICULTY	☻
EQUIPMENT	Baking paper and baking tray
TOOLS	

INGREDIENTS

7g easy action dried yeast
300ml lukewarm water
Pinch of sugar
450g strong white bread flour
Pinch of salt

For the tiger paste:

30g rice flour
1 tsp fast action dried yeast
1 tsp caster sugar
50ml lukewarm water
2 tsp walnut oil

METHOD

▸ Put the yeast and a little of the warm water and sugar into a bowl and set aside for about 10 minutes until it is foamy.

▸ Pour the flour into the bowl with the yeast mixture, add the rest of the water and attach the dough hook.

▸ Add a little salt and set the machine to a slow speed, gradually increasing the speed to medium when the flour and water are incorporated.

▸ Let the machine run for 8-9 minutes then remove from the bowl and cover with a damp cloth. Leave in a warm place for about an hour, or until doubled in volume.

▸ Heat the oven to 200°C and line a baking tray with baking paper.

▸ Attach the K beater and make the paste by mixing together the rice flour, yeast, sugar and water on a low speed. Turn it up to high and pour in the walnut oil. Mix it well and set aside.

▸ Shape the dough into a round loaf and place onto the baking tray. Brush the top with the tiger paste and leave to rest for 30 minutes.

▸ **Bake for 25-30 minutes.** Remove from the oven and leave to cool on a wire rack.

RUSSIAN RYE TREACLE BREAD

THIS TRADITIONAL RUSSIAN BREAD IS DELICIOUS WITH SMOKED SALMON.

SERVES	4
PREP TIME	10 minutes plus 1 hour 30 minutes for rising and rest
COOKING TIME	30 minutes
TEMPERATURE	240°C / Gas 9
DIFFICULTY	●●
EQUIPMENT	Loaf tin
TOOLS	

INGREDIENTS

450g rye flour
450g plain flour
7g easy action dried yeast
45g caster sugar
500ml warm water
2 tbsp treacle
2 tsp of salt

METHOD

▸ Attach the K beater and mix all the ingredients, apart from the salt, on a low speed for around 4 minutes or until everything is well incorporated. Add the salt and mix for another 30 seconds.

▸ Remove the K beater and attach the dough hook. Knead on a medium speed for 10 minutes, scraping down the bowl every so often.

▸ Remove the bowl and cover with a damp cloth, leave to rise in a warm place for an hour or until doubled in size.

▸ Put the mix into a loaf tin, or shape into a loaf and place on a lined baking tray. Leave for a further 30 minutes.

▸ Brush the top with water and smooth the surface with a spatula. **Bake for 45 minutes at 240°C,** remove from the oven and leave to cool on a wire rack.

BRIOCHE

SERVES	Makes 1
PREP TIME	50 minutes plus 2 hours rising time
COOKING TIME	1 hour 15 minutes
TEMPERATURE	200℃ / Gas 6
DIFFICULTY	◖◖
EQUIPMENT	Loaf tin
TOOLS	

INGREDIENTS

7g easy action dried yeast
60ml warm milk
450g plain flour
1 tbsp salt
4 eggs, beaten
250g butter
30g caster sugar

To brush:

1 egg, beaten with 2 tbsp milk

METHOD

▶ Add the yeast and milk to the bowl and leave for 5 minutes.

▶ Add the flour, salt and eggs and attach the dough hook. Knead on a low speed for 5 minutes.

▶ Turn the speed up to medium and knead for a further 10 minutes until you have a smooth, elastic dough.

▶ Take the dough out of the bowl and set aside. Remove the dough hook and attach the K Beater and mix together the butter and caster sugar until creamy.

▶ Add the dough and beat together until well incorporated and the dough is shiny and comes away from the bowl.

▶ Remove the bowl and cover with a damp cloth. Leave to rise in a warm place for a couple of hours.

▶ Attach the dough hook and knock the dough back on a low speed for a couple of minutes. Remove from the bowl, cover and refrigerate overnight.

▶ Heat the oven to 200℃ and grease a loaf tin.

▶ Remove the dough from the fridge and divide into two pieces, one piece half the size of the other. Shape the larger piece into a loaf and place in the tin. With the smaller second piece divide into 6 individual balls and press each one on top of the loaf.

▶ Brush the top with beaten egg and milk, leave to rise for an hour until doubled in size.

▶ **Bake the brioche for 15 minutes.** Turn the heat down to 160℃ and **cook for a further 50-60 minutes.**

▶ Remove from the oven and leave to cool in the tin for 5 minutes before turning out onto a wire rack.

CORIANDER AND PEPPER NAAN BREAD

NAAN BREAD IS A WONDERFULLY SOFT, PILLOWY BREAD WITH LOVELY CHARRED PARTS. THE KEY IS GETTING THE GRILL AS HOT AS POSSIBLE AND USING A REALLY HOT CAST IRON GRIDDLE PAN TO RECREATE THE HIGH TEMPERATURES OF THE TRADITIONAL TANDOOR.

SERVES	4
PREP TIME	10 minutes plus rising
COOKING TIME	30 minutes
DIFFICULTY	⊙
EQUIPMENT	Cast iron skillet or flat pan
TOOLS	

INGREDIENTS

7g easy action dried yeast
60ml warm milk
500g plain flour
1 tsp sugar
2 tsp nigella seeds (black cumin)
400ml warm milk
45ml natural yoghurt
1 egg, beaten
1 tsp ground coriander
Sunflower oil
2 tbsp melted butter
2 tbsp chopped coriander to garnish
Salt and pepper for seasoning

METHOD

➤ Mix the yeast with a little warm milk in a bowl and leave for 10 minutes.

➤ Attach the dough hook and add the flour, sugar and nigella seeds to the bowl. Add the yeast and knead well on a medium speed.

➤ With the motor running, pour in the warm milk and natural yoghurt, then add the egg and a pinch of salt. Knead for 10 minutes on a low speed.

➤ Remove the bowl and cover with a damp cloth and leave somewhere warm to rise for an hour. Add a tablespoon or two of flour if too wet.

➤ Generously flour a work surface and break off fist sized balls of dough and roll them out into a large teardrop shape, about 1cm thick. Sprinkle with the ground coriander, salt and freshly ground black pepper. Leave to rise for a further 30 minutes while you put a cast iron skillet or flat pan on a high heat.

➤ Add a little oil to the pan and put one of the breads in. **Cook for a minute** until the top starts to blister and brown a little. Remove from the pan and keep warm in a preheated grill while you repeat the process with the others, making sure to keep the pan very hot.

➤ Brush with melted butter, sprinkle over the fresh coriander and serve with a curry of your choice.

HOMEMADE PITTA BREAD

SERVES	6
PREP TIME	15 minutes plus 1 hour rising
COOKING TIME	2 minutes per pitta
DIFFICULTY	●
EQUIPMENT	Rolling pin, skillet or flat pan and baking paper
TOOLS	

INGREDIENTS

7g easy action dried yeast
1 tbsp sugar
300g strong flour
150ml lukewarm water
2 tbsp olive oil
2 tsp salt

METHOD

▷ Add the yeast and a little warm water with the sugar to the bowl, when it starts to foam add the flour. Attach the dough hook and knead on a low speed, gradually adding the water and oil while it kneads.

▷ Add the salt and knead for a further 5 minutes.

▷ Remove the bowl, cover with a cloth and leave to rise in a warm place for at least an hour.

▷ Turn out of the bowl onto a floured surface and knock the air out of it by kneading a little.

▷ Divide the dough into six balls. You could add some chilli flakes, pepper or cumin seeds to some of them if you like.

▷ Roll each ball out to about 15cm.

▷ Wipe a cast iron skillet/flat pan with a little oil and heat it until very hot, but not smoking. **Cook each bread for a couple of minutes** on either side until they start to puff up.

▷ Pile on greaseproof paper and serve. You can keep them warm wrapped in a cloth in a low oven if needed.

MINI BURGER BUNS

SERVES	12
PREP TIME	10 minutes plus 1 hour rising
COOKING TIME	20 minutes
TEMPERATURE	190°C / Gas 5
DIFFICULTY	
EQUIPMENT	Baking tray
TOOLS	

INGREDIENTS

250ml milk
30g butter, melted
1 egg
400g plain flour
7g easy action dried yeast
60g caster sugar
A pinch of salt
1 egg beaten

METHOD

▶ Heat the oven to 190°C.

▶ Add the milk, butter and egg to the bowl and attach the whisk. Whisk together on a low speed.

▶ Remove the whisk and attach the dough hook and add the flour, yeast, sugar and salt. Knead on a medium speed for 6 to 8 minutes.

▶ Cover the bowl with a cloth and leave to rise in a warm place for an hour, or until doubled in size.

▶ Remove the dough from the bowl and form into 12 buns, place on a baking tray and leave to rise for another 20 minutes.

▶ Brush with some beaten egg and **bake in the oven for about 20 minutes,** or until golden and springy. Leave to cool.

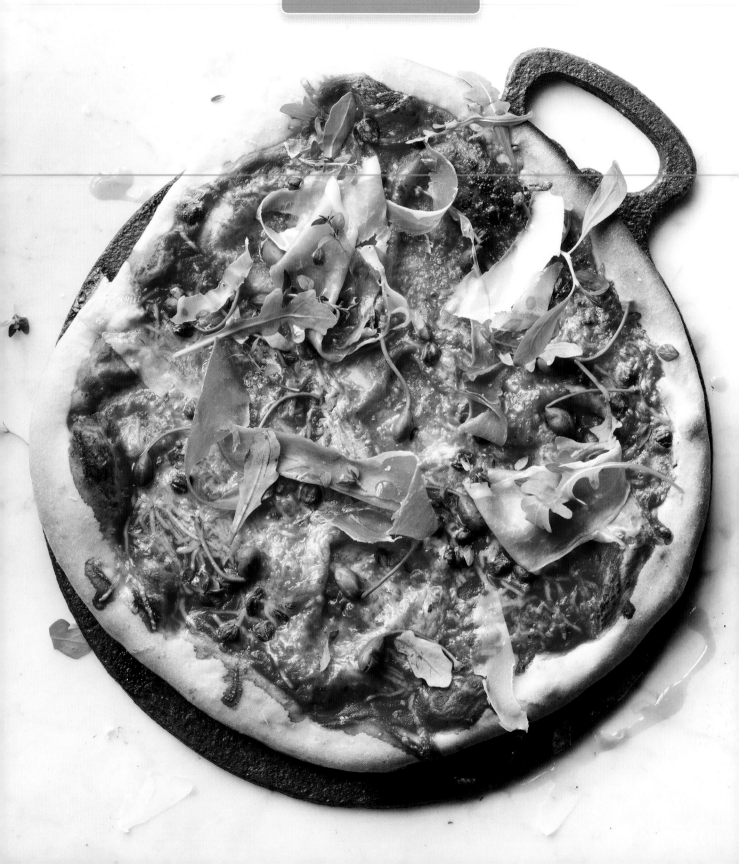

PARMA HAM, ROCKET, CAPER AND PARMESAN PIZZA

LEAVING THE DOUGH TO PROVE FOR 24 HOURS REALLY HELPS DEVELOP A DELICIOUS FLAVOUR AND CRUST.

SERVES	4
PREP TIME	5 minutes plus 24 hours proving and rising
COOKING TIME	12 minutes
TEMPERATURE	250°C / Gas 9
DIFFICULTY	☻
TOOLS	

INGREDIENTS

For the dough:

500g strong white flour, preferably type '00'

7g dry yeast

1 tbsp sugar

100ml lukewarm water

1 tbsp salt

30ml olive oil

For the topping:

Tomato purée

150g Mozzarella, grated or Emmental, torn

4 tbsp capers

75g Parmesan

4 slices parma ham

100g rocket leaves

A drizzle of olive oil

Salt and pepper

METHOD

▸ *To make the dough:* add the flour, yeast and sugar to the bowl. Attach the dough hook and knead on a low speed slowly adding the water. Knead well for a few minutes then add the salt.

▸ Turn the speed up to medium, add the oil and knead for 10 minutes.

▸ Put in a large bowl and cover with a damp cloth. Leave to rise for 2 hours, then knock the air out of the dough. Leave to rise for a further 2 hours, then cover with oiled clear film and put in the fridge for up to 20 hours.

▸ Remove the dough from the fridge and divide into four balls and roll out thinly.

▸ Preheat the oven to 250°C.

▸ Spread tomato purée over the base allowing a 2cm gap around the edge, sprinkle over the cheese and give it a twist of salt and pepper.

▸ Sprinkle over the capers and half the parmesan and **cook directly on the oven shelf for 12 minutes,** or until the cheese is bubbling and the crust golden.

▸ Remove from the oven and lay over the parma ham and rocket leaves. Drizzle with olive oil and serve.

CHICKEN, LEEK AND HAM PIE

SERVES	4
PREP TIME	25 minutes plus resting
COOKING TIME	60 minutes
TEMPERATURE	180°C / Gas 4
DIFFICULTY	👁️👁️
EQUIPMENT	Pie/pastry dish and baking beans
TOOLS	

INGREDIENTS

For the pastry:

150g chilled unsalted butter, cubed
300g plain flour
2 eggs, 1 beaten
Pinch of salt
30ml water

For the filling:

1 onion
1 leek
1 clove of garlic
6 chicken thighs, skinless and boneless
200ml vermouth or white wine
200ml double cream
125g cubed ham
1 tbsp chopped tarragon

For the roux:

50g butter
50g plain flour
200ml chicken stock
Olive oil
Salt and pepper to season

METHOD

▸ Heat the oven to 180°C.

▸ Add the butter, flour, whole egg and salt to the bowl, attach the K Beater and mix together on a medium speed until it comes together in a ball. Add a splash of water if necessary.

▸ On a floured surface roll out the pastry into a small rectangle, wrap in clear film and leave to rest in the fridge for half an hour.

▸ Finely slice the onion, leeks and garlic and gently cook in a little olive oil until translucent and soft. Season well.

▸ Cube the chicken and add to the pan. **Cook for about 8 minutes.** Pour in the vermouth and stir well. Bring to the boil and reduce by half, turn down the heat and add the cream. Simmer for 5 minutes and add the cubed ham and tarragon.

▸ In another saucepan make a roux by melting the 50g of butter in a pan and stir in the 50g of plain flour. Mix well and cook for a couple of minutes on a low heat, stirring all the time, then add the chicken stock a little at a time, then add the chicken and ham mixture. Stir well.

▸ Remove the pastry from the fridge and roll out to 1cm thick. Cut off enough to make a lid and reserve. Line a pastry dish with the pastry and place baking paper on top with baking beans and **bake in the oven for 10 minutes.**

▸ Remove from the oven and take out the beans and baking paper, brush with beaten egg and **return to the oven for a further 5 minutes.**

▸ Remove from the oven and fill the dish with the chicken and ham mixture, place the reserved pastry on top, crimping the edges over the pie. Make a little hole in the middle for the steam to escape. Glaze the lid with the beaten egg and **cook in the oven for 35-40 minutes** until the pastry is crisp and golden.

▸ Remove from the oven and leave to cool a little and serve.

CROISSANTS AND PAINS AU CHOCOLAT

THE KEY TO A GOOD CROISSANT IS A VERY FLAKY PASTRY. THEY ARE VERY EASY TO MAKE, THEY JUST NEED A LITTLE LOVE AND TIME.

SERVES	Makes 6
PREP TIME	35 minutes plus rising
COOKING TIME	15 minutes
TEMPERATURE	200°C / Gas 6
DIFFICULTY	● ● ●
EQUIPMENT	Rolling pin, baking tray
TOOLS	

INGREDIENTS

7g easy action dried yeast
60g sugar
250ml warm milk
500g plain flour plus a little extra for dusting
A pinch of salt
275g butter chilled

For brushing:

1 egg, beaten

70% cocoa dark chocolate for pains au chocolat

METHOD

▸ Put the yeast and 5g of the sugar in a bowl with a little of the milk. Leave for 3-4 minutes until foaming.

▸ Add the flour, salt and the remaining 55g of the sugar to the bowl, attach the dough hook and mix until combined.

▸ Add the yeast mixture and the rest of the milk to the bowl and knead until the flour comes together and has absorbed all the milk. Be careful not to mix it too much or the dough will be heavy.

▸ Leave the mixture in the bowl and put it in a warm place to rise for an hour.

▸ On a floured work surface roll out the dough into a large rectangle, always rolling in one long direction.

▸ Dot the whole surface with butter and fold into three, from the top down. Roll out and dot again with butter. Fold into three again and leave the dough in the fridge overnight.

▸ Roll the dough into a rectangle 45cm x 15cm and cut into triangles (roughly 20cm x 10cm). Roll up from the point and curve into crescents. Leave to rise for another hour.

▸ Brush each one with the beaten egg and place on a greased baking tray. **Bake in the oven at 220°C for about 15 minutes,** or until golden.

▸ To make pains au chocolat, cut rectangles of pastry and lay two strips of chocolate side by side down the middle. Fold the edges in and roll into a cylinder. Glaze with the egg and bake as croissants.

NORWEGIAN SKILLINGSBOLLER

LET THE DOUGH RISE SLOWLY OVERNIGHT AND YOU WILL HAVE DELICIOUS, SOFT CINNAMON BUNS FOR BREAKFAST.

SERVES	Makes 12
PREP TIME	20 minutes
COOKING TIME	25 minutes
TEMPERATURE	200°C / Gas 6
DIFFICULTY	✿
EQUIPMENT	Rolling pin, baking tray, baking paper
TOOLS	

INGREDIENTS

250g butter
400ml milk
250g caster sugar
2 tbsp ground cinnamon
1 tsp ground cardamom
600g plain flour
7g easy action dried yeast
A pinch salt
2 tbsp granulated sugar

METHOD

▷ Melt half the butter in a pan and add half the milk, half the caster sugar, half the cinnamon and all of the cardamom and dissolve.

▷ Add the flour and yeast and attach the dough hook, knead until combined. Add the butter mixture and the remaining milk and knead until you have a slightly sticky dough. Add the salt and knead a little more on a medium speed until the dough comes away from the edge of the bowl. You may need to add a little more milk and flour to achieve this.

▷ Cover the bowl with a damp cloth and leave to rest in a warm place for an hour.

▷ Heat gently the remaining butter, caster sugar and cinnamon in a pan, until the butter is softening but not melted. Stir well and leave to cool.

▷ Split the dough in two and roll one piece out into a 50cm x 25cm rectangle. Spread the cinnamon butter over and roll the dough away from you into a tight cylinder.

▷ Place seam side down on a chopping board and slice into 3cm rings. Place face up on the baking tray leaving 2cm between each one. Repeat the process with the remaining dough.

▷ Leave to rise for one hour, or overnight in the fridge.

▷ Remove from the fridge and heat the oven to 200°C. **Cook the buns for about 20 minutes** or until lightly golden and puffy. Sprinkle granulated sugar over them, allow to cool for five minutes and serve.

THICK PANCAKES WITH MAPLE SYRUP

SERVES	4
PREP TIME	10 minutes
COOKING TIME	10 minutes
DIFFICULTY	☻
EQUIPMENT	Flat pan
TOOLS	

INGREDIENTS

250ml buttermilk
2 tbsp vegetable oil
2 eggs
200g flour
2 tsp baking powder
1 tsp bicarbonate of soda
1 tbsp sugar

To serve:

Maple syrup
Butter
Icing sugar to dust

METHOD

▸ Attach the K beater and pour the milk, oil and eggs into the bowl and mix together on a medium speed.

▸ Add the flour, baking powder, soda and sugar to the bowl mix gently until everything is just combined. It should still be a little lumpy.

▸ Heat a flat pan with a little oil and spoon in enough batter to make an 8cm pancake. **Cook for a couple of minutes** until bubbles start to appear on the surface.

▸ Flip over with a spatula and cook for a further 2 minutes.

▸ Serve a few piled up on plate with a drizzle of maple syrup and butter then dust with icing sugar.

GRUYÈRE GOUGÈRE

SERVES	6-8 (makes 14)
PREP TIME	15 minutes
COOKING TIME	25 minutes
TEMPERATURE	200°C / Gas 6
DIFFICULTY	⊖
EQUIPMENT	Baking tray and baking paper
TOOLS	

INGREDIENTS

125g unsalted butter
125ml milk
1 tsp Dijon mustard
1 teaspoon salt
1 teaspoon paprika
125ml water
225g plain flour
4 large eggs
150g Gruyère cheese grated

METHOD

▶ Preheat the oven to 200°C and line a large baking tray with baking paper.

▶ Add the butter, milk, mustard, salt, paprika and water to a saucepan and bring to the boil. Reduce the heat and mix in the flour. Cook for a further 3 minutes stirring constantly with a wooden spoon until the mixture comes together away from the edges of the pan.

▶ Attach the K beater and pour the warm mixture into the bowl. Mix for 1 minute on a medium speed.

▶ Add the eggs one at a time, waiting until each egg is fully incorporated before adding the next.

▶ Add the grated cheese and continue to mix well.

▶ Using a tablespoon, drop spoonfuls of the batter onto the baking sheet in a circle, leaving a small gap between each, so as they rise they join together but retain their individual shape.

▶ **Cook for 8-10 minutes** then reduce the heat to 170°C and **cook for a further 15 minutes,** or until the gougère is golden.

▶ Remove from the oven and quickly poke each segment with a toothpick to let the steam out.

▶ Leave to cool for a few minutes and serve.

CHEESE AND PAPRIKA PASTRY TWISTS

A QUICK AND EASY SNACK WHICH GOES WELL WITH AN APERITIF.

SERVES	8
PREP TIME	5 minutes plus resting
COOKING TIME	15 minutes
TEMPERATURE	200℃ / Gas 6
DIFFICULTY	❷
EQUIPMENT	Baking tray
TOOLS	

INGREDIENTS

400g strong white flour
100g plain white flour
500g unsalted butter, chilled and diced
5g salt
300ml very cold water
1 tbsp cider vinegar
50g Parmesan cheese
200g Jarlsberg cheese
1 tbsp paprika
Salt and pepper

METHOD

▶ Attach the dough hook and add both flours and butter to the bowl. Gently knead them together until combined (about 2 minutes on a low speed), then add the salt, water and cider vinegar and mix on a medium speed until it comes together as a ball. The vinegar helps soften the dough for easier rolling.

▶ Flour the work surface and lightly roll out. Fold in on itself and repeat, dusting with flour as you go, until you have a large rectangle of pastry. Then cut in half, and roll out each rectangle to roughly 20cm x 35cm. Wrap in clear film and chill in the fridge for 20 minutes.

▶ Heat the oven to 200°C.

▶ Remove both rectangles from the fridge, roll them out again then fold in on themselves as before, wrap and chill for another 20 minutes.

▶ Roll both rectangles out to 55cm x 25cm and sprinkle over the Parmesan and Jarlsberg and sprinkle one rectangle with paprika and a twist of pepper and salt. Then cover with the other rectangle of pastry.

▶ Cut into strips and roll into twists. **Bake in the oven for about 12 minutes** until golden. Leave to cool on wire racks and serve.

LAPSANG SOUCHONG MUFFINS

THE SMOKY FLAVOUR OF THE TEA
COMPLEMENTS THE LIGHT SWEETNESS OF THE
MUFFINS AND MAKES FOR AN INTERESTING
TWIST ON A CLASSIC.

SERVES	12
PREP TIME	10 minutes
COOKING TIME	20 minutes
TEMPERATURE	180°C / Gas 4
DIFFICULTY	◉
EQUIPMENT	Baking tray or muffin tin
TOOLS	

INGREDIENTS

2 eggs
100ml vegetable oil
100ml milk
200g caster sugar
375g self-raising flour
1 tsp baking powder
1 tsp fine lapsang souchong tea leaves
A pinch salt
Icing sugar to dust

METHOD

▸ Heat the oven to 180°C and line a baking
tray or muffin tin with 12 muffin cases.

▸ Attach the K beater add the eggs, oil and
milk and mix on a medium speed, slowly add
the sugar and mix until dissolved.

▸ Add the remaining ingredients and mix well
until fully combined and smooth.

▸ Fill each case two thirds full and **bake for
about 20 minutes** until risen and golden.

▸ Dust with icing sugar and serve.

CHOCOLATE AND CHILLI BROWNIES WITH COGNAC

SERVES	12
PREP TIME	20 minutes
COOKING TIME	20-25 minutes
TEMPERATURE	180°C / Gas 4
DIFFICULTY	●
EQUIPMENT	Square/rectangular baking tin, baking paper
TOOLS	

INGREDIENTS

250g dark chocolate (80%)
50g milk chocolate
150g butter
150g brown sugar
150g golden caster sugar
4 eggs
100g plain flour
A pinch of salt
2 tbsp chilli powder
2 tbsp Cognac
4 tbsp cocoa powder

METHOD

▶ Heat the oven to 180°C and line a square/rectangular baking tin with baking paper.

▶ Put a pan of water on to boil and gently melt the dark chocolate, milk chocolate and butter together in a heatproof bowl above the water. Stir occasionally and take it off the heat as soon as it is melting together.

▶ Attach the whisk and pour in the melted chocolate, both sugars, the eggs and whisk on a high speed for 5 minutes.

▶ Remove the whisk and attach the K beater. Gradually add the flour with the machine running on a low speed. Add the salt, chilli powder, Cognac and cocoa, mix well until fully combined.

▶ Pour the mix into the baking tray and **bake for 20 minutes,** until they are firm, yet soft and squidgy. Remove from the oven and leave to cool. Dust with cocoa and cut into 12 squares. Store in an airtight tin.

PENNSYLVANIA DUTCH APPLE CRUMBLE

SERVES	4
PREP TIME	25 minutes plus 1 hour resting
COOKING TIME	35-40 minutes
TEMPERATURE	200°C / Gas mark 6
DIFFICULTY	☻
EQUIPMENT	4 small pastry dishes
TOOLS	

INGREDIENTS

For the pastry:

175g plain flour
85g butter (cubed)
30-45ml water
Pinch of salt

For the filling:

1 tsp cinnamon
1 tsp nutmeg
Zest and juice of 1 lemon
150g plain flour
1 tsp caster sugar
1kg apples, peeled and cored

For the crumble mixture:

200g unsalted butter (cubed)
1 tsp cinnamon
1 tsp nutmeg
200g light brown sugar
200g wholemeal flour

METHOD

▶ *To make the pastry:* Add the flour, salt and butter to the bowl. Attach the K beater and mix on a low speed until it resembles bread crumbs.

▶ With the machine still running slowly add the water until a dough forms. Remove from the bowl and wrap in clear film, leave to chill in the fridge for 30 minutes.

▶ Remove the dough from the fridge and roll onto a floured surface. Line four small pastry dishes with the pastry and leave to rest in the fridge for 30 minutes.

▶ *To make the filling:* Add the cinnamon, nutmeg, zest and juice of the lemon, plain flour and caster sugar. Attach the K beater and mix until combined, remove from the bowl and reserve.

▶ *To make the crumble mix:* Add the butter, cinnamon, nutmeg, sugar, and wholemeal flour. Attach the K beater and mix on a medium speed until the mixture comes together, remove from the bowl and reserve.

▶ *To assemble the crumble:* Remove the pastry dishes from the fridge, slice the apples and divide between the dishes. Add the reserved filling mixture and top with the crumble mix.

▶ **Bake in the oven for 35-40 minutes,** until golden. Serve warm with a little cream.

KENWOOD
Original Recipe

CHOCOLATE TART
WITH VANILLA CREAM

SERVES	6-8
PREP TIME	30 minutes
COOKING TIME	40 minutes plus chilling
TEMPERATURE	200°C / Gas 6
DIFFICULTY	☻
EQUIPMENT	20cm tart tin, baking beans
TOOLS	

INGREDIENTS

For the base:

250g plain flour
125g unsalted butter
125g sugar
1 egg

For the filling:

100ml milk
300ml double cream
200g dark chocolate
50g white chocolate
2 eggs
1 egg white

For the vanilla cream:

250ml double cream
1 tbsp vanilla extract
Icing sugar to dust

METHOD

➤ Heat the oven to 200°C. Grease a 20cm tart tin.

➤ *For the base:* attach the K beater and add the flour, butter, sugar and egg. Mix on a medium speed until it comes together, remove from the bowl, flatten slightly, cover with clear film and chill for half an hour in the fridge.

➤ Remove the pastry from the fridge and roll out to 5mm thick, lay it into the tart tin cover with baking paper and fill with baking beans/ rice. Bake in the oven for 10 minutes, turn the oven to 180°C, remove the beans, trim the pastry and bake for a further 10 minutes. Remove from the oven and leave to cool.

➤ *For the filling:* heat the milk and cream together in a pan and pour over the top of the dark and white chocolate to melt it.

➤ Attach the whisk and add the whole eggs and egg white, with the machine running at a medium speed whisk in the melted chocolate, mix until combined.

➤ Pour the mixture over the tart base and **bake in the oven for 35 minutes,** until the mixture is set, but with a good wobble. Cool and dust with icing sugar.

➤ *For the vanilla cream:* whisk together the cream and vanilla until you have soft, pillowy peaks. Serve with the chocolate tart.

YOGHURT, CARDAMOM AND ELDERFLOWER BUNDT CAKE

DELICATE AND MOIST, THIS CAKE MAKES A GREAT TREAT ON A SUMMER AFTERNOON WITH A CUP OF EARL GREY TEA.

SERVES	6-8
PREP TIME	15 minutes
COOKING TIME	45 minutes
TEMPERATURE	180°C / Gas 4
DIFFICULTY	
EQUIPMENT	Bundt tin
TOOLS	

INGREDIENTS

125g unsalted butter, softened
250g caster sugar
1 tbsp ground cardamom
1 tsp vanilla extract
1 egg
2 tbsp elderflower cordial
250g self-raising flour
1 tsp baking powder
250ml natural yoghurt

METHOD

▸ Heat the oven to 180°C and grease a bundt tin.

▸ Add the butter, sugar, cardamom and vanilla to the bowl. Attach the K beater and mix together on a medium speed until light and fluffy. Gradually add the egg and elderflower. Mix until smooth.

▸ Remove the K beater and attach the creaming beater and fold in the flour (with baking powder) and natural yoghurt in alternate spoonfuls.

▸ Pour the cake mix into the tin and **bake for 35 minutes,** or until a knife poked in comes out clean.

LEMON POLENTA CAKE

THIS IS A VERY SIMPLE CAKE THAT TAKES
MINUTES TO PREPARE. SERVE IT WITH A
CHILLED GLASS OF LIMONCELLO TO GET THE
FULL ITALIAN EXPERIENCE.

SERVES	8
PREP TIME	10 minutes
COOKING TIME	45 minutes
TEMPERATURE	160°C / Gas 3
DIFFICULTY	⊘
EQUIPMENT	25cm spring form cake tin
TOOLS	

INGREDIENTS

250g butter
250ml caster sugar
3 eggs
150g polenta
175g ground almonds
Juice and zest of 2 lemons
1 tsp baking powder
A pinch salt

METHOD

▸ Heat the oven to 160°C. Grease and line a
25cm springform cake tin.

▸ Attach the K beater, add butter and sugar
to the bowl and cream together using a
medium speed.

▸ Then add the remaining ingredients and mix
together until you have a smooth batter.

▸ Pour into the cake tin.

▸ **Bake in the oven for about 45 minutes**
until slightly risen and golden brown. If you
see it browning too much, cover the top with
some foil.

▸ Remove from the oven and leave to cool a
little. Dust with icing sugar and serve.

LEMON AND LIME PIE

SERVES	8
PREP TIME	25 minutes
COOKING TIME	35 minutes plus chilling
TEMPERATURE	190°C / Gas 5
DIFFICULTY	☺
EQUIPMENT	19cm spring form cake tin
TOOLS	

INGREDIENTS

For the base:

15 digestive biscuits
90g unsalted butter, melted
Zest of 1 lime

For the filling:

4 egg yolks
400g tin of condensed milk
Zest and juice of 2 lemons
Zest and juice of 3 limes
Reserve some of the zest for decoration

For the meringue:

3 egg whites
150g caster sugar

METHOD

▸ Preheat the oven to 190°C and grease a 19cm spring form cake tin.

▸ *For the base:* Add the biscuits to the bowl and attach the K Beater, mix on a high speed until they are fine breadcrumbs.

▸ Add the melted butter and lime zest and mix until combined. Press the mixture into the cake tin and bake in the oven for 10 minutes, remove and leave to cool slightly.

▸ *For the filling:* Remove the K beater and attach the whisk. Add the egg yolks and whisk on a medium speed for 1 minute. With the machine on a low speed pour in the milk, zest and juice and whisk for a further minute. Pour the mixture on top of the biscuit base and reserve.

▸ Clean the bowl and whisk the egg whites until stiff peaks form. Add the sugar one tablespoon at a time and keep whisking until glossy and stiff. Spoon onto the top of the pie.

▸ **Bake in the oven for 20-25 minutes** until slightly set and the meringue is golden.

▸ Sprinkle with lime zest to decorate and chill in the fridge for about four hours.

MACAROONS

THESE ARE A LIGHT AND DELICATE TREAT, AND
VERY PRETTY TO LOOK AT. YOU CAN USE ANY
FOOD COLOURING YOU LIKE AND CAN CHANGE
THE FILLING TO MATCH. TRY CHOCOLATE
BUTTERCREAM WITH BROWN FOOD COLOURING
OR PEPPERMINT FLAVOURED WHIPPED CREAM
WITH GREEN FOOD COLOURING.

SERVES	8
PREP TIME	10 minutes
COOKING TIME	20 minutes
TEMPERATURE	160°C / Gas 3
DIFFICULTY	●●
EQUIPMENT	Piping bag, baking tray
TOOLS	

INGREDIENTS

4 egg whites
75g caster sugar
1 tsp pink food colouring
125g ground almonds
225g icing sugar
A pinch salt
12 tbsp raspberry conserve
100ml cream

METHOD

▸ Heat the oven to 160°C and line a baking tray
with baking paper.

▸ Attach the whisk and add the egg whites,
caster sugar and food colouring. Whisk on a
high speed until you have stiff peaks.

▸ Remove the whisk and attach the creaming
beater. Slowly fold in the ground almond,
icing sugar and salt on a low speed. Mix
until smooth and syrupy then scrape into a
piping bag.

▸ Pipe 3cm discs of the mixture onto the tray,
leaving a couple of centimetres between each
one. Tap the tray hard on the work surface to
help prevent the tops cracking and **bake for
about 20 minutes** or until they come away
easily from the paper.

▸ Leave to cool.

▸ Add the cream to the bowl and attach
the whisk. Whisk until you have soft peaks.
Remove the whisk and add the creaming
beater, add the jam and mix until combined.

▸ Sandwich the macarons together with the
jam mix and serve.

RED VELVET CAKE

SERVES	6-8
PREP TIME	25 minutes plus 30 minutes chilling time
COOKING TIME	25-30 minutes
TEMPERATURE	180°C / Gas 4
DIFFICULTY	◑ ◑
EQUIPMENT	x2 15cm round cake tins
TOOLS	

INGREDIENTS

For the cake:

120g butter

300g sugar

2 eggs

1 tsp Vanilla extract

250g self-raising flour

1tsp baking powder

1 tbsp cocoa powder

240ml butter milk

2 tbsp red food colouring

For the buttercream:

125g butter, softened

125g cream cheese

1 tbsp vanilla extract

200g icing sugar

50g almonds to decorate

METHOD

▸ Heat the oven to 180°C and grease and line two 15cm round cake tins.

▸ Add the butter and sugar to the bowl, attach the creaming beater and mix on a medium speed until pale and fluffy. Add the eggs and vanilla extract and mix on a medium speed until they are fully incorporated.

▸ Remove the creaming beater and attach the K beater, add the flour, baking powder and cocoa powder a bit at a time, mixing on a slow speed between each addition until fully incorporated.

▸ Measure out the buttermilk in a separate jug and add the red food colouring, stir together until red. Add the red mix to the bowl a little at a time and mix on a medium speed until you have a smooth deep red batter.

▸ Divide the mixture between the two cake tins and **bake for 25-30 minutes,** or until a knife inserted into the sponge comes out clean. Remove from the oven, leave in the tin for 10 minutes then turn out to cool completely on wire racks.

▸ Meanwhile, make the butter cream icing. Add the butter, cream cheese and vanilla extract to the bowl, attach the creaming beater and mix together on a medium speed until smooth. Gradually add the icing sugar and mix until you have a creamy icing. Chill for 30 minutes.

▸ To decorate, place one of the cake halves on a plate and cover the top and sides with the icing. Put the other half on top and cover the top and sides of that with the remaining icing. Smooth over and sprinkle with almonds.

DRINKS AND SOUPS

THIS CHAPTER UTILISES THE BLENDER ATTACHMENT WHICH IS IDEAL FOR DRINKS, SOUPS, MILKSHAKES, SMOOTHIES, COCKTAILS, SAUCES AND ICE CRUSHING.

There are a variety of blenders available, from thermoresist glass that can withstand thermal shock to stainless steel, so you can select one that suits you. Blenders are really easy to use and guarantee you the freshest possible outcomes.

As well as a naughty cocktail or two you can have a warming hearty soup or a healthy smoothie to kick start your day. It is so easy and these recipes should give you the inspiration to create many more combinations.

FROZEN MARGARITA

SERVES	4
PREP TIME	5 minutes
DIFFICULTY	
TOOLS	

INGREDIENTS

140ml tequila
60ml triple sec
Juice of 2 limes
20 ice cubes
Icing sugar
Salt

METHOD

▶ Add the tequila, triple sec and lime juice to the blender and give it a quick blend.

▶ Add the ice cubes and blend until crushed.

▶ Pour into martini glasses that have had their rims dipped in sugar and salt, serve.

PISCO SOUR

SERVES	4
PREP TIME	4 minutes
DIFFICULTY	
TOOLS	

INGREDIENTS

2 egg whites
50g icing sugar
Juice of 2 limes
200ml Pisco (or use white tequila)

METHOD

▶ Attach the blender and add the egg whites and sugar, blend on a high speed.

▶ With the motor running pour the lime juice and pisco through the filler lid.

▶ Add some ice and stir well.

▶ Pour into 4 tall glasses and serve.

APPLE AND ORANGE VIRGIN JULEP

SERVES	4
PREP TIME	5 minutes
COOKING TIME	5 minutes
DIFFICULTY	
TOOLS	

INGREDIENTS

1 sprig of mint, a few leaves reserved for garnish
1 orange, peeled and quartered, zest reserved for garnish
100g caster sugar
200ml water
500ml apple juice
Ice cubes

METHOD

▶ Attach the blender and blend the mint, orange and sugar together. Put in a pan and add the water. Bring to the boil then **simmer for 5 minutes.** Strain and set aside.

▶ Fill four glasses with ice, add the apple juice and top with the mint and orange syrup. Garnish with mint leaves and the zest.

LEMONADE

SERVES	6
PREP TIME	5 minutes
DIFFICULTY	●
TOOLS	

INGREDIENTS

800ml cold water
3 tbsp sugar
6 ice cubes
1 lemon

METHOD

▸ Attach the blender and add the water, sugar, ice cubes and whole lemon.

▸ Blend on a high speed for 1 minute.

▸ Pour the lemonade through a sieve into a jug and serve.

STRAWBERRY AND RASPBERRY ICE DRINK

SERVES	4
PREP TIME	10 minutes
DIFFICULTY	●
TOOLS	

INGREDIENTS

20 ice cubes
500g strawberries
500g raspberries
100ml hot water
50g caster sugar
A few mint sprigs

METHOD

▸ Add the ice to the blender six cubes at a time with a little hot water and leave to melt slightly.

▸ Add the fruit and sugar and mix on a high speed.

▸ Pour into glasses and serve with the mint leaves to garnish.

TROPICAL FRUIT SMOOTHIE

SERVES	4
PREP TIME	5 minutes
DIFFICULTY	●
TOOLS	

INGREDIENTS

1 pineapple
1 mango
1 banana
1 passion fruit
1 kiwi
1 melon
500ml natural yoghurt

METHOD

▸ Peel all the fruit and cut into chunks. Attach the blender and blend everything together until smooth.

▸ Divide between four glasses and serve.

FRENCH ONION SOUP

SERVES	4
PREP TIME	20 minutes
COOKING TIME	60 minutes
DIFFICULTY	😊😊
TOOLS	

INGREDIENTS

8 white onions, peeled
2 tbsp butter
Olive oil
2 sprigs of thyme
2 tbsp flour
1.5 litre beef stock
Salt and pepper to season
4 slices of baguette
60g Gruyère cheese, grated

METHOD

▸ Thinly slice the onions and heat the butter and oil in a heavy based pan. Add the onions and thyme sprigs, season and stir well. Turn the heat down to low. **Cook for about 40 minutes,** stirring often until the onions have caramelised and are sweet and dark brown.

▸ Heat the grill to high.

▸ Add the flour to the pan, stir well and cook for a minute more.

▸ Stir in the stock, **bring to the boil and simmer for 5 minutes.** Attach the blender and blend half of the soup then return to the pan. Season well and keep warm

▸ Toast one side of the baguette slices then add the cheese to the other and melt under the grill with a little salt and pepper.

▸ Serve the soup in bowls with the bread on top.

PEA AND HAM HOCK SOUP

SERVES	4-6
PREP TIME	15 minutes
COOKING TIME	90 minutes
DIFFICULTY	
TOOLS	

INGREDIENTS

2 ham hocks
2 carrots
1 onion
1 bay leaf
1 sprig of thyme
1 rosemary sprig
1 Maris Piper potato
1 litre water
500 petits pois peas
Salt and pepper to season
1 stick of celery, leaves set aside

METHOD

▸ Add all the ingredients except the peas to a large pan. Bring to the boil then reduce to a simmer and **cook for 80 minutes,** skimming the surface regularly until the ham hock is cooked and the meat its tender. Remove the hocks, take off the meat, shred with a fork and set aside.

▸ Add the peas to the liquid base and attach the blender, blend on a medium speed. Return to the pan, add the meat and return to a gentle heat for ten minutes.

▸ Taste, adjust the seasoning and serve with some chopped celery leaves.

PRAWN AND CRAB BISQUE

SERVES	6
PREP TIME	25 minutes
COOKING TIME	60 minutes
DIFFICULTY	
TOOLS	

INGREDIENTS

2 onions
½ a head of garlic
5 carrots
½ a bunch of celery sticks
Olive oil
2 whole chillies
2 tbsp of turmeric
2 tbsp of ground cumin
2 tbsp of paprika
1½ tbsp of ground coriander
1 tbsp of cayenne pepper
2 tbsp of ground ginger
A large pinch of saffron
225g crab meat
20 or so prawn heads and shells
½ a glass of white wine
10ml brandy
½ a tube of tomato puree
2 tins of chopped tomatoes
A handful of rice
½ a litre of water
Salt
6 tbsp crème fraîche
4 tbsp dill leaves

METHOD

▶ Slice the onions, garlic, carrots, celery and chillies.

▶ Heat some olive oil in the largest pan you have and cook the vegetables gently while you mix the spices and saffron together in a bowl.

▶ Wrap the prawns in a tea-towel and hit them with a rolling pin until you have smaller broken bits. Add the prawn and the crab meat to the pan, turn up the heat and give everything a good stir for a few minutes.

▶ De-glaze the pan with the white wine and let it reduce down. When there is not much liquid left, pour in the brandy and set fire to it with a match. Let the alcohol burn off and throw in the spices, add the tomato puree and stir well.

▶ Pour in the chopped tomatoes, mix everything around and bring to the boil. Pour in the rice and the water and season well with salt. Boil for five minutes, then cover and turn down the heat. **Simmer gently for 40 minutes.**

▶ Pour the soup in batches into the blender and blend on a high speed until fine. Before serving pour the mixture through a sieve to catch any remaining prawn shells.

▶ Pour into serving bowls and serve with a dollop of crème fraîche mixed with chopped dill.

WHITE GAZPACHO

SERVES	4-6
PREP TIME	15 minutes
COOKING TIME	10 minutes
DIFFICULTY	◑ ◑
TOOLS	

INGREDIENTS

5 slices stale white bread, crusts removed
100ml sherry vinegar
500ml hot chicken or vegetable stock
2 cucumbers
200g green, seedless grapes
200g blanched, skinless almonds
2 cloves of garlic
Salt and pepper to season
100ml olive oil

METHOD

▸ Add the bread and vinegar to the stock and leave to soak.

▸ Attach the blender and add the remaining ingredients apart from the olive oil to the blender. Blend well and slowly add the bread and stock.

▸ With the motor running slowly pour in the olive oil until you have a smooth creamy liquid. Taste and adjust the seasoning.

▸ Chill in the fridge until cold and serve with crusty bread and a glass of dry sherry.

SPICED BUTTERNUT SQUASH SOUP

SERVES	4
PREP TIME	10 minutes
COOKING TIME	25 minutes
DIFFICULTY	
TOOLS	

INGREDIENTS

1 tbsp ground coriander

1 tbsp ground turmeric

1 tbsp ground cumin seeds

1 clove of garlic

1 medium sized butternut squash, peeled and cut into long, narrow pieces

3 red chillies, sliced and seeds removed

2 tbsp olive oil

Salt and pepper to season

750ml chicken or vegetable stock

METHOD

▶ Slice the butternut squash and chillies and chop the garlic.

▶ Heat some oil on a medium heat in a large frying pan and add the squash, chillies and garlic. Season with a little salt and pepper and add the ground spices.

▶ Cook until the squash is soft and starting to turn golden on the edges.

▶ Add the chicken stock to the pan. Bring to a boil then reduce the heat to a simmer and **cook for 5 minutes.**

▶ Leave to cool for a few minutes, attach the blender attachment and blend.

▶ Check the seasoning and serve with a little olive oil and the ground spices.

BORSCHT

SERVES	4
PREP TIME	10 minutes
COOKING TIME	60 minutes
DIFFICULTY	😊😊
TOOLS	

INGREDIENTS

8 spring onions
4 gherkins
4 cooked and peeled beetroot
400g potatoes
1 onion
250g diced beef shin
1 litre beef or chicken stock
2 bunches of dill
200ml sour cream
Salt and pepper to season

METHOD

▸ Slice the spring onions, gherkins, beetroot, potato and onions, reserve.

▸ Heat some oil in a large saucepan and season and brown the beef all over. Add the sliced vegetables and stock and bring to the boil. Reduce the heat to a simmer, **cover and cook for about an hour.**

▸ Attach the blender and blend in batches, removing as much meat as possible. Taste and adjust the seasoning.

▸ Chop the dill and divide the soup between four bowls.

▸ Top with a spoonful of sour cream and the onions, gherkins and dill. Serve with rye bread.

ENTERTAINING

MAKING RESTAURANT QUALITY FOOD ACCESSIBLE FOR THE HOME KITCHEN IS ANOTHER GREAT FEATURE OF THE KENWOOD CHEF.

Being able to finely slice or dice large quantities of vegetables exactly the same size in next to no time helps with the presentation side, while being able to blend hot purées, strain stocks and pass sauces gives that extra quality touch that will impress your guests.

Some of these recipes may seem a little complicated, but with the right ingredients, a little practice, and the wide range of the Kenwood Chef's handy functions and attachments, it really is a case of restaurant quality food made easy!

LOBSTER AND PROSECCO RISOTTO

SERVES	4
PREP TIME	30 minutes plus resting
COOKING TIME	5 minutes
DIFFICULTY	☺☺
EQUIPMENT	Saucepans, 4 soup bowls
TOOLS	

INGREDIENTS:

1 800g lobster, whole

200ml double cream

A pinch of salt

800ml fish stock

1 onion

Olive oil

200g risotto rice, I would suggest carnaroli

175ml Prosecco

50g butter, chilled and cubed

2 tbsp parsley, chopped

METHOD

▶ Bring a large pan of salted water to the boil and **cook the lobster for 12 minutes.** Remove from the pan and cool quickly in cold water.

▶ Carefully remove all the flesh from the claws and tail, slice into pieces and reserve.

▶ Attach the blender and add the lobster shell, cream and a little salt. Pulse until finely ground.

▶ Once ground, pass the lobster cream mixture through a sieve, capturing any un-blended shell. Reserve the mixture.

▶ Heat the fish stock in a saucepan and keep on a gentle simmer.

▶ Remove the blender and attach the food processor with the knife blade and finely chop the onion, reserve.

▶ Heat a large deep pan with a little olive oil and add the risotto rice and chopped onion. **Cook for a couple of minutes,** stirring constantly to toast all the risotto grains.

▶ Add the Prosecco and reduce until almost gone. Pour in a ladleful of the fish stock and stir well until fully absorbed. Keep doing this until all the stock is used and the rice is al dente. Taste and adjust the seasoning.

▶ Add the butter and chopped parsley and mix thoroughly. Gently stir in the reserved lobster meat, **cover and leave for 5 minutes.**

▶ Meanwhile, gently warm the lobster cream in a saucepan, divide between four bowls and add the risotto.

▶ Serve with a glass of prosecco.

CHEF'S TIP

To keep the lobster from curling run a skewer lengthwise through the centre of the lobster tail meat.

PICKLED RADISH AND MUSHROOM WITH SWEET CURED HERRING

SERVES	4
PREP TIME	20 minutes plus curing (8 hours or overnight)
DIFFICULTY	◉ ◉
EQUIPMENT	Large dish
TOOLS	

INGREDIENTS

1 carrot
2 tbsp caster sugar
Chopped dill
4 100g herring fillets
30g salt
16 round radishes
2 fennel stalks
2 spring onions
150g caster sugar
6 tbsp rice wine vinegar
1 jar of keta (salmon eggs)

METHOD

➤ Attach the food processor with the slicing disc and slice the carrot, reserve.

➤ Cure the herring by sprinkling the fillets with a pinch of salt and 2 tbsp caster sugar. Place the fish in a large dish with the chopped carrot and dill. Cover and leave in the fridge for at least 8 hours, overnight would be better to infuse the flavours.

➤ With the food processor still attached slice the radish, fennel stalks and spring onions. Add them to a bowl and pour over the sugar and rice wine vinegar. Stir gently and leave to pickle for half an hour.

➤ Rinse, pat dry and slice each herring fillet into three pieces. Place the pickled vegetables on plates and top with the herring pieces. Add a teaspoon of keta to each one and garnish with a little dill.

Get Attached!

QUICKLY AND EFFORTLESSLY SLICE VEGETABLES WITH THE **FOOD PROCESSOR ATTACHMENT.**

See page **106**

TUNA CARPACCIO WITH SALSA VERDE

THIS IS AN ELEGANT STARTER BURSTING WITH FLAVOUR AND VERY EASY TO PREPARE. THE SALSA VERDE CAN BE MADE THE DAY BEFORE GIVING YOU MORE TIME WITH YOUR GUESTS. FREEZING THE TUNA A LITTLE MAKES IT MUCH EASIER TO SLICE THINLY.

SERVES	4
PREP TIME	15-20 minutes
DIFFICULTY	●
EQUIPMENT	Frying pan
TOOLS	 

INGREDIENTS

For the salsa verde:

2 small bunches basil
1 large bunch coriander, including stems
1 large bunch parsley
1 small bunch mint
1 clove garlic, chopped
2 tbsp capers
2 tbsp Dijon mustard
Juice of 1 lemon
3 tarragon leaves
6 black olives
50ml olive oil
50ml rapeseed oil
Salt to season

For the tuna carpaccio:

4 tbsp black peppercorns
1 tsp fennel seed
1 tsp salt
400g tuna loin
Juice of one lemon
A handful of rocket leaves to garnish

METHOD TO MAKE THE SALSA VERDE

➤ Attach the blender and add all the ingredients apart from the oils. Blend on a high speed for a minute, until the ingredients are chopped, but still have some texture.

➤ Turn the blender onto a low speed and slowly pour in the oils until the consistency is a thick cream. Adjust the seasoning and keep in an airtight jar in the fridge for up to five days.

METHOD TO MAKE THE TUNA CARPACCIO

➤ In a dry frying pan lightly toast the peppercorns and fennel seeds.

➤ Attach the compact chopper/grinder, add the toasted seeds with the salt and grind on a medium speed until a fine powder.

➤ Rub the powdered spices over the tuna and wrap tightly in clear film, place in the freezer for half an hour.

➤ Remove the tuna from the freezer and slice as thinly as possible.

➤ Arrange between four plates, squeeze over some lemon juice and dress with the salsa verde and a few rocket leaves to garnish.

SEARED SCALLOPS WITH CURRIED APPLE AND LEMON OIL

SCALLOPS GO VERY WELL WITH SWEET AND SHARP FLAVOURS, SO THE COMBINATION OF LIGHTLY SPICED APPLE AND LEMON OIL IS A WINNER. THE HERB CRUMBS ADD A PLEASING CRUNCH TO THE SOFTNESS OF THE SHELLFISH.

SERVES	4
PREP TIME	30 minutes
COOKING TIME	10 minutes
TEMPERATURE	160°C / Gas 3
DIFFICULTY	❷
EQUIPMENT	Baking tray, baking paper, saucepan
TOOLS	

INGREDIENTS

For the lemon oil:

75ml olive oil
2 sticks of lemon grass
Zest and juice of 1 lemon

For the scallops:

2 apples, cored
1 tsp ground turmeric
1 tsp ground cumin
1 tsp ground fennel
1 tsp ground coriander
½ tsp chilli powder
1 tsp fresh parsley
1 tsp fresh thyme leaves
2 slices of bread, stale or well dried out in the oven
2 tbsp butter
12 large scallops
Salt and pepper

METHOD

➤ Preheat the oven to 160°C and line a baking tray with baking paper.

➤ Mix the ground spices together in a bowl, slice the apples and lay them onto the baking tray. Sprinkle the spice mix over the apples and **place the tray in the oven for 30 minutes.**

➤ Add the lemon oil ingredients to the compact chopper/grinder and grind on a high speed, reserve.

➤ Remove the compact chopper/grinder and attach the blender, add the herbs, bread and a pinch of salt. Blend together on a high speed until you have bread crumbs, reserve.

➤ Heat a saucepan and add the butter, when foaming add the scallops to the pan. Season and spoon over the butter as you **cook them for 1 minute.** Turn them over and **cook for a further minute,** again spooning over the butter. Remove from the pan and drain on kitchen paper.

➤ Divide the apple slices between 4 plates, top with the scallops and drizzle over the reserved lemon oil mix. Sprinkle over the reserved bread crumbs to finish, and serve.

CHEF'S TIP

Scallops cook very quickly, so put them in the pan clockwise and remove them in the same order you put them in. This way, they will all be evenly done.

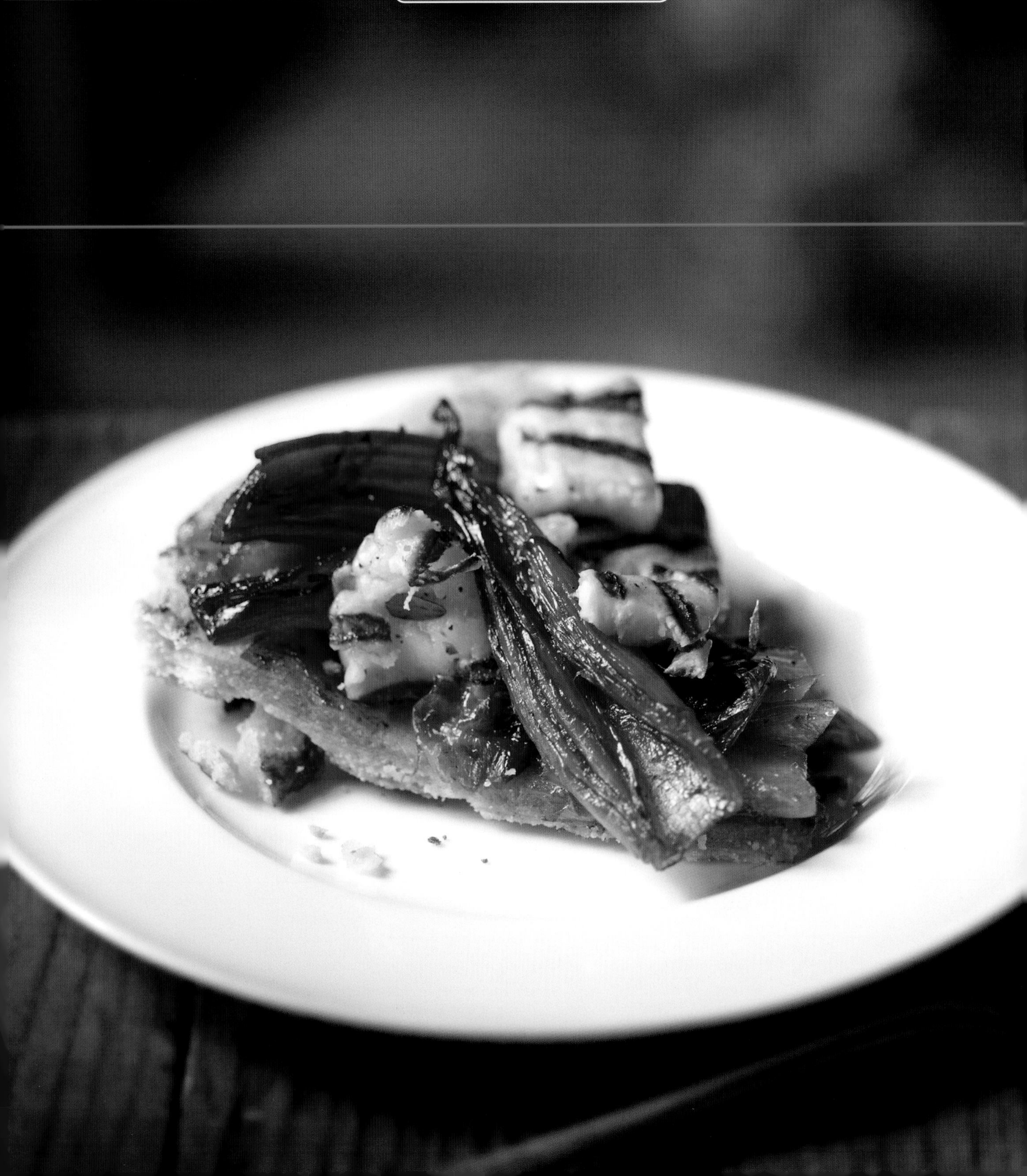

SHALLOT TART WITH CHARGRILLED HALLOUMI

SERVES	4
PREP TIME	15 minutes, plus 30 minutes resting time for the pastry
COOKING TIME	45 minutes
TEMPERATURE	180°C / Gas 4
DIFFICULTY	☺ ☺
EQUIPMENT	Baking tray, baking paper, shallow pan
TOOLS	

INGREDIENTS

For the pastry:

150g chilled unsalted butter, cubed

300g plain flour

1 egg

pinch of salt

30ml water

For the filling:

100g butter

500g shallots, peeled and sliced

6 tbsp balsamic vinegar

100ml vegetable stock

4 tbsp brown sugar

4 thyme sprigs

1 block of halloumi

Zest of one lemon

1 tsp dried oregano

Salt and pepper to season

METHOD

▶ Preheat the oven to 180°C. Line a baking tray with baking paper.

▶ Add the butter, flour, egg and salt to the bowl, attach the K beater and mix together on a medium speed until it comes together in a ball.

▶ On a floured surface roll out the pastry into a small rectangle, wrap in clear film and leave to rest in the fridge for 1/2 an hour.

▶ Melt butter in a pan and add the shallots until nicely browned.

▶ Add the vinegar and stock, turn over the shallots and **cook for five more minutes** on a very low heat. Sprinkle with the sugar and thyme sprigs.

▶ Remove the shortcrust pastry from the fridge, lightly sprinkle a work surface with flour and roll out to about 1/2cm thick. Place onto the baking tray and spread over the shallot mixture. Fold in the edges and **cook in the oven for 45 minutes.**

▶ Attach the food processor with the slicing disc and slice the halloumi, sprinkle with lemon zest, oregano and pepper then fry in a hot shallow pan with a little olive oil until charring.

▶ Remove the tart from the oven, leave to cool a little and serve with the halloumi.

CHEF'S TIP

....

You could replace the shallots with red onion and use feta instead of halloumi.

....

PUMPKIN AND AMARETTO RAVIOLI WITH HERB BUTTER

THE ALMOND FLAVOUR OF AMARETTO REALLY COMPLEMENTS THE PUMPKIN IN THE RAVIOLI.

SERVES	4
PREP TIME	30 minutes, plus 30 minutes resting time for the pasta dough
COOKING TIME	40 minutes
TEMPERATURE	200°C / Gas 6
DIFFICULTY	🍴🍴
EQUIPMENT	Roasting dish, saucepan
TOOLS	

INGREDIENTS

For the pasta dough:

500g strong type '00' flour

4 eggs beaten

2 tbsp water (if necessary)

Salt to season

For the filling:

500g pumpkin flesh

1 tbsp olive oil

Salt and pepper

2 cloves of garlic, unpeeled

15g amaretti biscuits

1 egg, beaten

Semolina flour for dusting

100g butter

Chopped herbs: parsley, rosemary, thyme or herbs of your choosing

Zest and juice of a lemon

Salad leaves and parmesan (optional)

METHOD

▶ Add the flour and salt to the bowl and attach the dough hook. With the machine running slowly add the eggs. Add the water and slowly increase the speed until a dough is formed. Add more water/flour if mixture is too dry or too wet.

▶ Remove the dough from the bowl and wrap in clear film. Leave to rest in the fridge for at least half an hour before using. You can freeze any left over for up to one month.

▶ Preheat the oven to 200°C.

▶ Attach the dicing attachment and dice the pumpkin flesh. Place the diced pumpkin into a roasting dish and add a tbsp of olive oil, salt and pepper and the 2 garlic cloves, **roast in the oven for 25-30 minutes,** until soft and golden.

▶ Remove the dicing attachment and attach the food processor with the knife blade, add the roasted pumpkin, amaretti biscuits and 2 tbsp of olive oil. Process on a medium speed until fairly smooth, reserve in the fridge.

▶ Remove the food processor and attach the flat pasta roller. Remove the dough from the fridge and divide it into four. Pat each one with your hands into a rectangle shape until the dough is thick enough to pass through the pasta roller - ensuring the pasta roller is set at no.1.

▶ Feed each one through the flat pasta roller several times adjusting the thickness to no. 8.

▶ Take one sheet of the rolled flat pasta and put a teaspoon of the reserved pumpkin mixture at intervals along the sheet. Brush around each spoonful of mixture with beaten egg, then lay another sheet of pasta on top.

▶ Press down around each filling to seal, then cut into ravioli with a knife or cookie cutter. Press out any excess air from each one, dust in a little semolina and set aside.

▶ Repeat the process with the other two pasta sheets.

▶ Bring a large pan of salted water to the boil.

▶ Melt the butter in a pan, add the chopped herbs and sauté until they start to crisp. Be careful to not burn them. Add the lemon zest and juice and turn off the heat.

▶ **Cook the ravioli in the salted boiling water for 2-3 minutes,** then drain. Pour the butter and herb mix over the cooked ravioli.

▶ Serve with parmesan and a good twist of black pepper and some soft salad leaves.

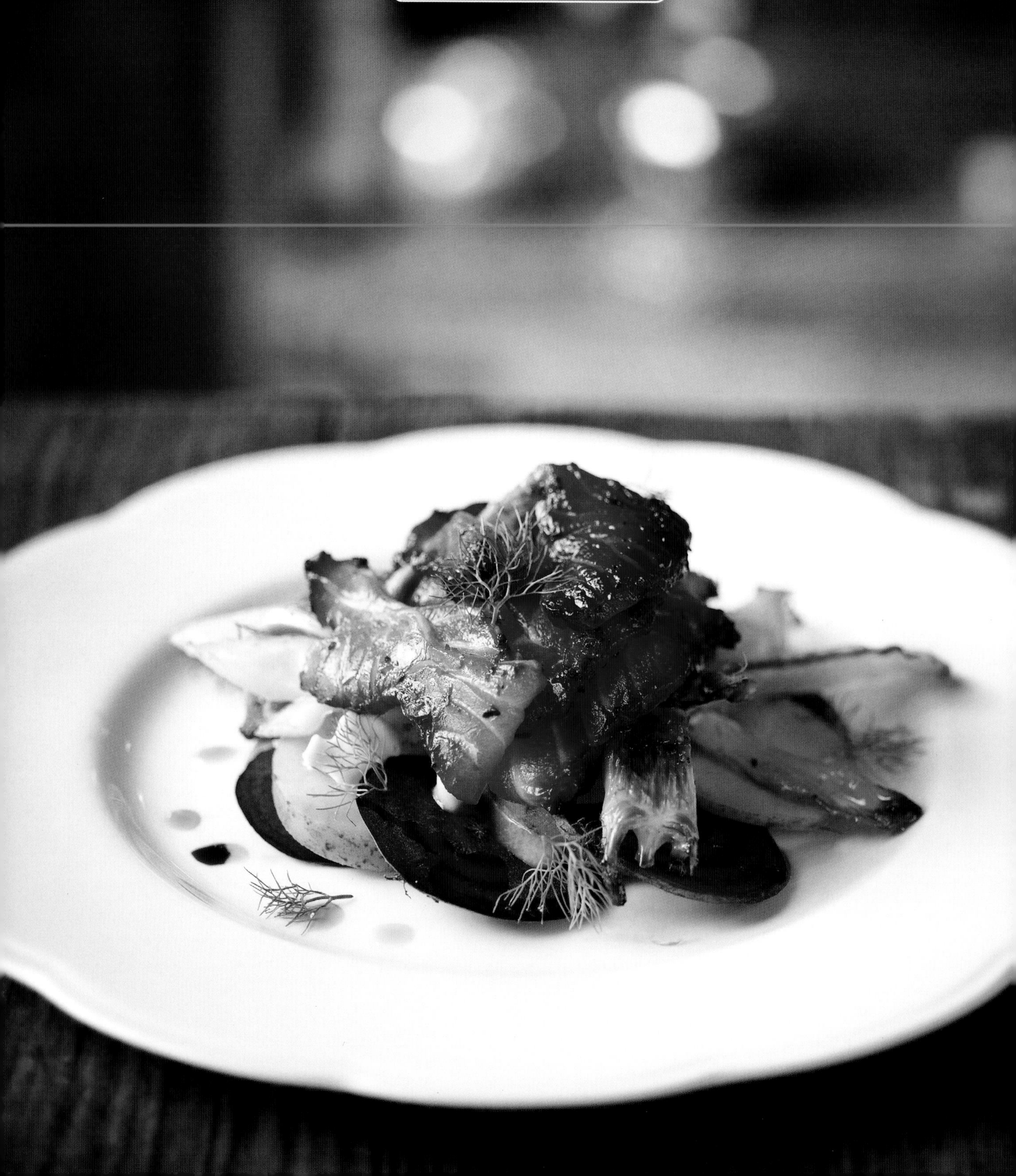

BEETROOT AND DILL CURED SALMON WITH ROAST FENNEL

SERVES	4
PREP TIME	3-4 days curing, 30 minutes
COOKING TIME	30 minutes
TEMPERATURE	180°C / Gas 4
DIFFICULTY	● ●
EQUIPMENT	Baking tray
TOOLS	

INGREDIENTS

150g salt
200g sugar
3 bunches of dill, stalks removed
2 tbsp red wine vinegar
4 raw beetroots
1 side of salmon
4 fennel bulbs
4 potatoes
Juice and zest of 1 lemon
Olive oil
Salt and pepper to season

METHOD TO MAKE THE CURE

▶ 3-4 days before you plan to serve your dish, attach the compact chopper/grinder with half of the salt, sugar, dill leaves and a splash of vinegar, grind on a medium speed. Repeat the process with the other half and reserve together in a bowl.

▶ Remove the compact chopper/grinder and attach the food processor with the grating disc, grate the beetroots. Add the grated beetroot to the reserved salt mixture (the cure).

▶ Line a baking tray with clear film and spread over some of the cure.

▶ Cut the salmon in half, widthways and lay (skin side down) onto the baking tray. Cover the salmon with the rest of the mixture, making sure it is completely covered.

▶ Fold the clear film from underneath and put some more over the top of the salmon, sealing it. Place a chopping board on top and a couple of small, full tin cans. Leave in the fridge for 3-4 days, draining off excess liquid every now and then.

METHOD TO MAKE THE DISH

▶ Preheat the oven to 180°C.

▶ Remove the salmon from the fridge, take off the skin and clean off the cure, leave it to come to room temperature for about half an hour, then slice finely.

▶ Attach the food processor with the slicing disc and slice the fennel bulbs and potatoes. Add the lemon juice to the slices and place on a baking tray drizzled with olive oil.

▶ **Cook in the oven for about 30 minutes,** or until starting to colour nicely, turning halfway through.

▶ Serve the sliced salmon with the cooked vegetables.

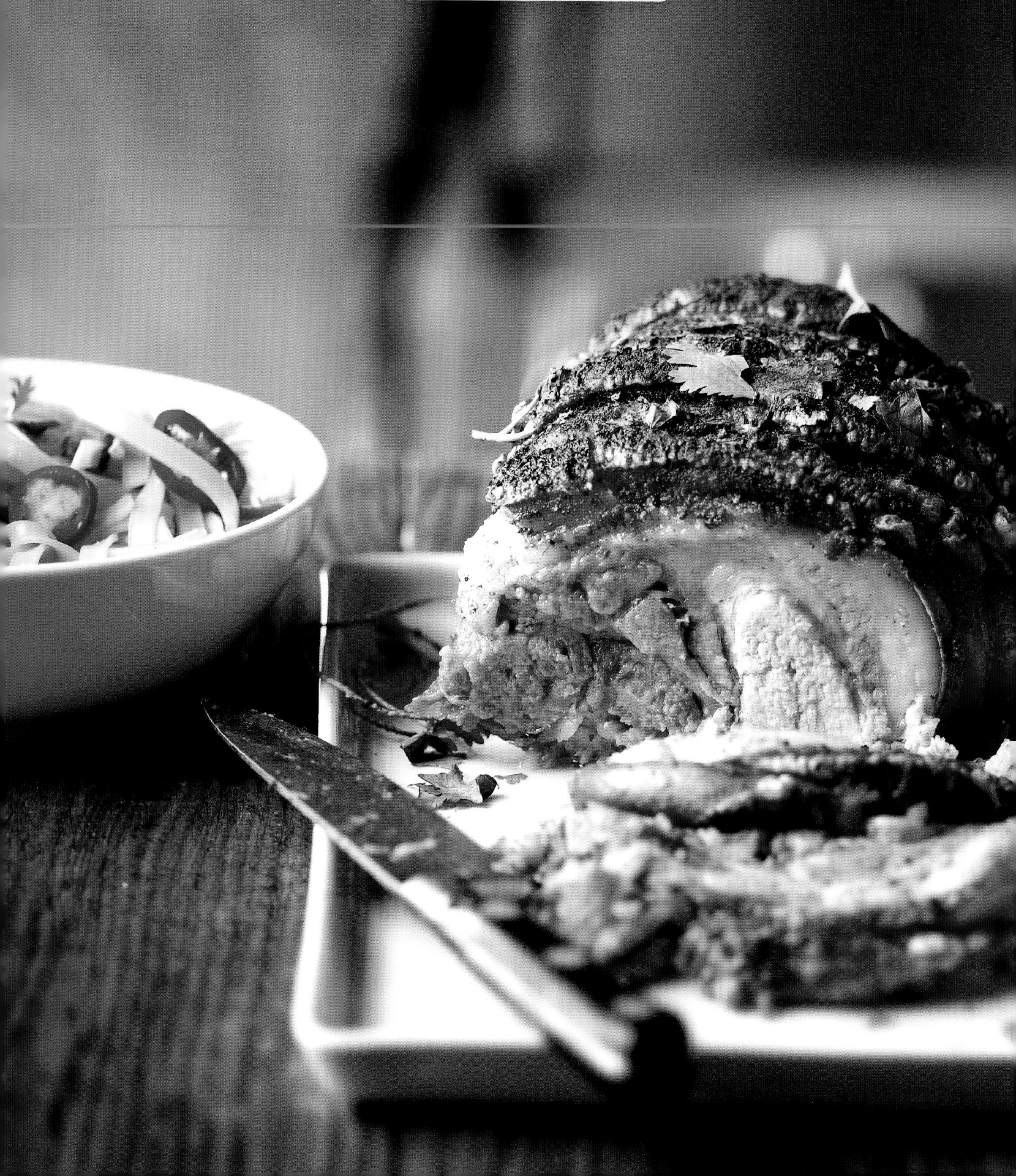

BRAISED PORK WITH CHERVIL, ANISE AND CHILLI NOODLES

THIS ASIAN-INSPIRED PORK DISH MAKES A GREAT SHARING PLATTER AND THE BRAISING MAKES IT TENDER AND MOIST. AND OF COURSE, EVERYONE LOVES A BIT OF CRACKLING, SO FINISHING IT UNDER THE GRILL GIVES IT THAT MOUTH-WATERING CRUNCH.

SERVES	4-6
PREP TIME	25 minutes, plus overnight for infusing flavours
COOKING TIME	160 minutes, plus 40 minutes resting
TEMPERATURE	220°C / Gas 7
DIFFICULTY	
EQUIPMENT	Roasting tray
TOOLS	

INGREDIENTS

For the pork:

2kg pork shoulder joint
3 star anise
2 tbsp fennel seeds
4 tbsp dried chervil
1 tbsp chilli powder
Salt and pepper
400ml chicken stock

For the noodles:

250g rice noodles
2 tbsp sweet chilli sauce
1 tbsp soy sauce
2 red chillies, sliced
4 spring onions, sliced
4 tbsp chopped coriander leaves

METHOD

‣ Score the fat on the pork. Put the shoulder in a deep sided roasting tray and pour over boiling water. This will help when it comes to the crackling. Drain and pat dry.

‣ Attach the compact chopper/grinder with the star anise and fennel seeds, grind then add the chervil, chilli powder and seasoning. Rub this mix all over the pork. Leave uncovered in the fridge overnight.

‣ Preheat the oven to 220°C.

‣ Heat the stock and pour it into the roasting tray **cook in the oven for 20 minutes.** Turn the heat down to 160°C and **cook for a further 140 minutes.** Remove from the oven and leave to rest.

‣ Preheat the grill to medium and grill the pork skin until bubbling.

‣ To make the noodles, put them in a large bowl and pour over boiling water. **Cover and leave for 10 minutes.** Drain and stir in the chilli sauce and soy sauce. Mix well then sprinkle over the chilli and spring onions.

‣ Slice the pork and arrange on a platter with the noodles. Sprinkle over the chopped coriander leaves and serve.

Get Attached!

CHOP AND GRIND HERBS AND SPICES FOR THE FRESHEST FLAVOURS WITH THE **COMPACT CHOPPER/GRINDER.**

See page 108

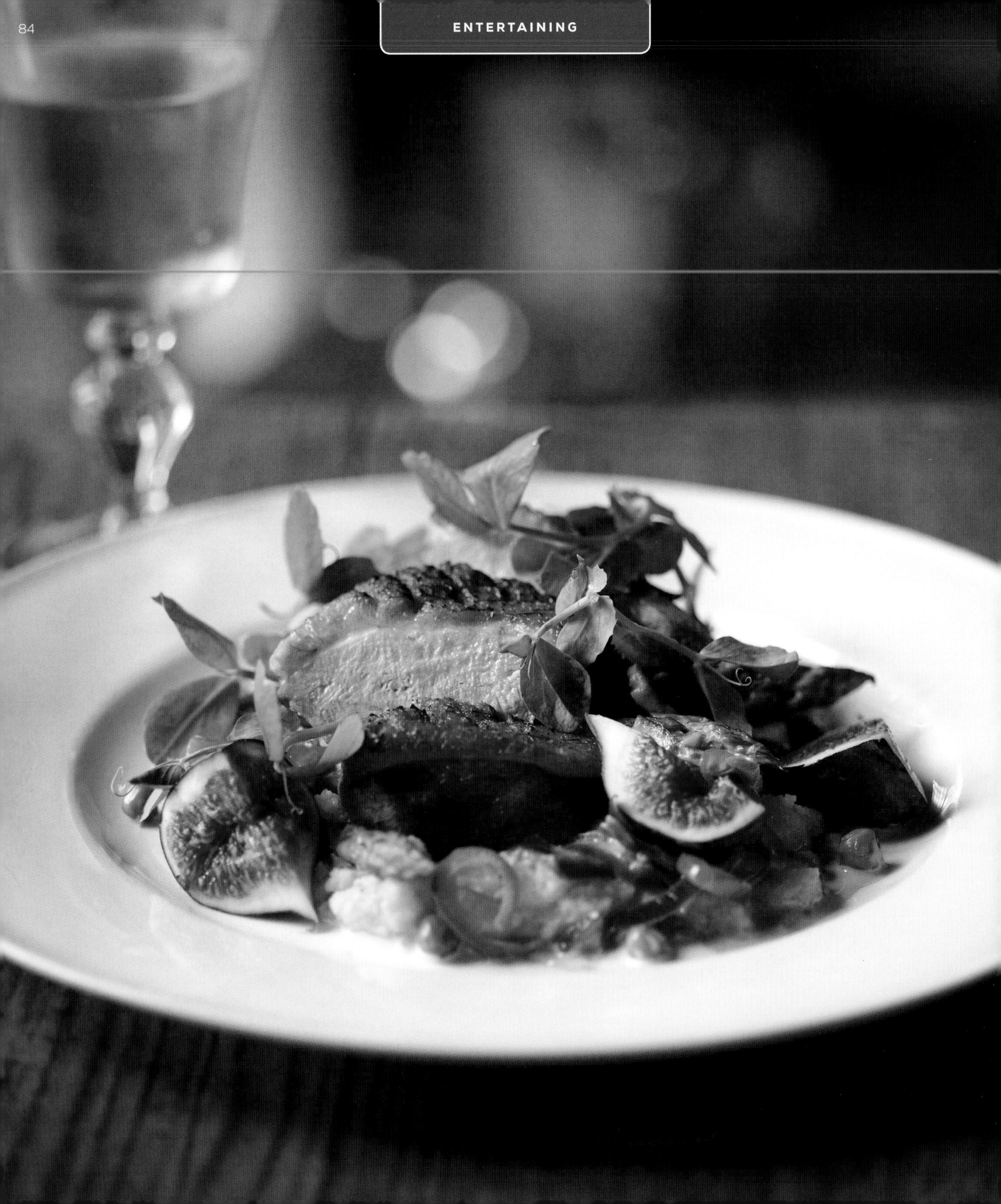

DUCK WITH ASPARAGUS, FIGS, PEA SHOOTS AND POLENTA

FRUIT IS A GREAT PARTNER WITH DUCK AND THE LIGHT SPRING FLAVOURS OF ASPARAGUS AND PEA GIVE THIS A REAL LIFT. THE POLENTA ADDS A COMFORTING CREAMINESS AND CRUNCH TO THE DISH.

SERVES	4
PREP TIME	25 minutes
COOKING TIME	10-15 minutes
TEMPERATURE	180°C / Gas 4
DIFFICULTY	☻ ☻
EQUIPMENT	Shallow pan, oven proof dish, saucepan
TOOLS	

INGREDIENTS

2 red onions
4 duck breasts
250g butter
200g polenta
600ml vegetable stock
100ml white wine
100g peas
16 asparagus spears
8 tbsp cream
50ml water
4 figs
150g pea shoots
Olive oil
Salt and pepper

METHOD

▸ Preheat the oven to 180°C.

▸ Attach the food processor with the slicing disc and slice the red onions, reserve.

▸ Score the fat on the duck, heat a shallow pan and place each duck breast skin side down and **cook gently for about 5-7 minutes** until turning golden. Turn over half way through and season.

▸ Take the meat from the pan and move to an oven proof dish, make sure you keep the pan with the duck fat.

▸ **Cook in the oven for 5 minutes** then remove, cover and leave to rest for five minutes.

▸ Meanwhile, heat a little of the butter in a saucepan and add the polenta. Stir, then add the vegetable stock. Bring to the boil and reduce to a simmer. When the stock is absorbed and the polenta is soft, stir in the remaining butter. Taste and adjust the seasoning, reserve.

▸ Re-heat the pan with the duck fat and sauté the reserved chopped onion. Season a little and pour in the vermouth. Reduce by half and add the peas and asparagus. **Cook for about 4 minutes** then add the cream and 50ml of water.

▸ Quarter the figs and diagonally slice each duck breast into three. Divide the polenta between the plates, top with the pea and asparagus mix and lay the duck on top.

▸ Place the figs around the duck and finish with some pea shoots and a drizzle of olive oil.

CHEF'S TIP

If asparagus is out of season swap for some long stemmed broccoli or leeks.

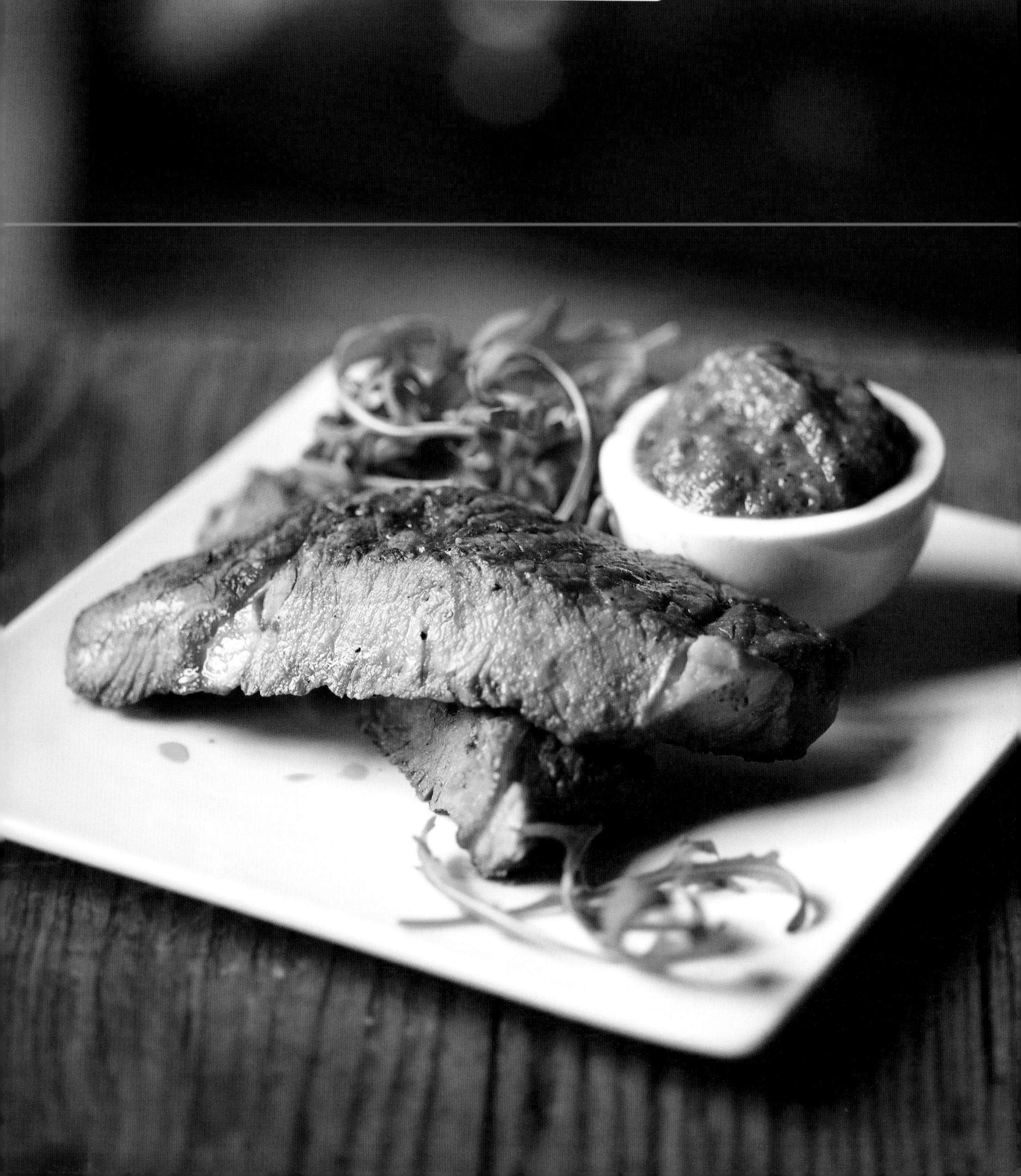

RIB-EYE STEAK WITH SMOKED AUBERGINE PURÉE AND ROCKET

SERVES	2
PREP TIME	10 minutes
COOKING TIME	45 minutes
TEMPERATURE	200°C / Gas 6
DIFFICULTY	
EQUIPMENT	Flat pan baking tray
TOOLS	

INGREDIENTS

2 rib-eye steaks, about 200g each, allowed to sit at room temperature for about 30 minutes

1 aubergine

1 tbsp olive oil

1 clove of garlic

2 tsp smoked paprika

Salt and pepper to season

1 bunch of salad leaves

1 tsp lemon juice

METHOD

➤ Preheat the oven to 200°C, and season the steaks.

➤ Place the aubergine and garlic onto a baking tray and cook in the oven **for about 35 minutes** or until it is soft.

➤ Attach the blender and add the olive oil, paprika, the cooked aubergine and a pinch of salt and pepper. Blend on a medium speed until you have a purée.

➤ Heat a flat pan until very hot and add the steaks. **Cook for 3 to 4 minutes** on each side for medium then allow to rest for a further 4 minutes.

➤ Serve with the aubergine purée and the salad leaves, dressed with a little oil and lemon juice.

Get Attached!

BLEND FRESH INGREDIENTS QUICKLY AND EFFORTLESSLY TO MAKE SOUPS, SAUCES, DIPS AND DRINKS.

See page 13

HERB CRUSTED RACK OF LAMB WITH ROAST VEGETABLES AND POMME PURÉE

THE HERB CRUST GIVES THE LAMB A STRONG VISUAL IMPACT AS WELL AS ADDING SUBLIME FLAVOUR TO THE MEAT. PAIRED WITH THE VEGETABLES AND POMME PURÉE THIS IS A VERY ELEGANT YET SIMPLE DISH.

SERVES	4
PREP TIME	25 minutes
COOKING TIME	45 minutes
TEMPERATURE	180°C / Gas 4
DIFFICULTY	😊😊
EQUIPMENT	Saucepan, roasting tray
TOOLS	

INGREDIENTS

For the pomme purée:
1kg potatoes (recommend floury type)
200g melted butter
150ml milk
175ml double cream
Salt to season

For the vegetables:
1 fennel bulb sliced
2 red onions, quartered
3 cloves of garlic
2 carrots, cut into batons
1 aubergine, cut into batons
Olive oil
Salt and pepper to season

For the lamb and herb crust:
4 slices of stale bread
2 tbsp chopped parsley
2 tbsp chopped rosemary
2 tbsp chopped mint
2 racks of lamb, with 6 bones on each
'French trimmed'
1 tbsp Dijon mustard
Salt and pepper to season
125ml white wine

METHOD TO MAKE THE POMME PUREE

▸ Preheat the oven to 180°C degrees.

▸ Peel the potatoes and cut into pieces and put in a pan of cold salted water. Bring to the boil and **cook for about 10 minutes,** or until nice and soft. Drain and leave to dry.

▸ Heat the butter, milk and cream in a pan.

▸ Attach the K beater and add the potatoes and cream, mix on a medium speed until the consistency is a creamy purée, reserve.

METHOD TO MAKE THE MAIN DISH

▸ Preheat the oven to 190°C.

▸ Put the vegetables on a roasting tray, drizzle with oil, season well and **roast for 20 minutes.**

▸ Attach the food processor with the knife blade. Add the bread and herbs, process on a medium speed until you have fine breadcrumbs.

▸ Score the lamb skin, season well and brown all over in a hot pan (keep the pan). Brush the mustard all over and coat with the bread crumb mix. Place the lamb on top of the vegetables in the oven. Deglaze the reserved pan and pour into the roasting tray. **Roast in the oven for a further 20 minutes.**

▸ Remove the lamb from the oven and let it rest for five minutes. Slice into cutlets and serve with the vegetables, the roasting juices and the pomme purée.

CHEF'S TIP

Make sure to let the lamb rest, covered in foil and a cloth for plenty of time. This helps all the fibres relax and reabsorb the juices giving tender meat.

RED SNAPPER
WITH PIPERADE

PIPERADE GOES BEAUTIFULLY WITH FISH.
IT IS ALSO MADE OF REALLY VIBRANT
COLOURS SO WILL CERTAINLY IMPRESS
YOUR GUESTS.

SERVES	4
PREP TIME	15 minutes plus 3-4 days curing
COOKING TIME	30 minutes
TEMPERATURE	180°C / Gas 4
DIFFICULTY	●
EQUIPMENT	Saucepan, shallow pan
TOOLS	

INGREDIENTS

4 200g red snapper fillets
A handful of parsley
1 lemon, quartered

For the Piperade:

1 large white onion
1 red pepper
1 green pepper
2 cloves of garlic
½ tsp smoked paprika
1 tin of plum tomatoes
Olive oil
Salt and pepper to season

METHOD

‣ Preheat the oven to 180°C.

‣ Attach the food processor with the slicing disc and slice the onion, peppers and garlic.

‣ Heat a saucepan with a little olive oil and gently cook the sliced onion, pepper and garlic until soft. Season with a little salt and add the smoked paprika. **Cook, stirring often on a medium heat** until the peppers are starting to soften.

‣ Add the tinned tomatoes to the pan and **cook for ten minutes.** Adjust the seasoning and keep warm while you cook the fish.

‣ Heat a shallow pan and **cook the 4 red snapper fillets for 5 to 6 minutes,** turning once.

‣ Serve each fillet with the piperade, sprinkle with chopped parsley and a wedge of lemon.

CHEF'S TIP

Ratatouille would work equally well with this dish, and you could use mullet instead of the snapper.

CHOCOLATE SPONGE WITH SALTED CARAMEL ICE CREAM

SERVES	4
PREP TIME	15 minutes, pre-freeze ice cream bowl for 24 hours
COOKING TIME	30 minutes
TEMPERATURE	200°C / Gas 6
DIFFICULTY	☻☻
EQUIPMENT	2 saucepans, 6 ramekin dishes / dariole moulds
TOOLS	

INGREDIENTS

For the salted caramel ice cream:

450g caster sugar
600ml double cream
2 tsp Maldon salt
250ml milk
4 egg yolks
1 tsp vanilla extract

For the fondants:

200g dark chocolate (70%)
150g sugar
150g butter
4 eggs, beaten
50g plain flour
2 tsp vanilla extract

METHOD TO MAKE THE SALTED CARAMEL ICE CREAM

‣ To make the ice cream, pre-freeze the frozen dessert maker bowl for 24 hours.

‣ Add 200g of the caster sugar to a saucepan and heat until melted.

‣ Once melted bring to the boil and continue cooking, stirring occasionally until it starts to turn golden. Add 200ml of the cream, stir well and cook until the caramelised sugar has dissolved. Add the salt and reserve.

‣ In another saucepan bring the milk to just below boiling and then turn off the heat.

‣ Attach the whisk, add the egg yolks and the remaining 250g of the caster sugar to the bowl. Whisk on a medium speed until pale and fluffy. Pour in the cooled milk and continuing to whisk until combined.

‣ Pour all of the mixture back into the saucepan and cook on a low heat for ten minutes, or until the mixture has thickened and coats the back of a wooden spoon.

‣ Turn the heat off and add the remaining cream (400ml). Stir well and add the vanilla extract.

‣ Chill in the fridge until cold.

‣ Remove the frozen dessert maker bowl from the freezer, attach the plastic bowl of the dessert maker and fit the freezer bowl inside it. Add the paddle and cover.

‣ With the machine running at a slow speed slowly pour the ice cream mix into the bowl through the feed chute. Mix in the frozen dessert maker for about half an hour, 20 minutes into mixing slowly add the reserved caramel mix.

‣ The ice cream can be eaten immediately or kept in the freezer for later.

METHOD TO MAKE THE CHOCOLATE FONDANT

‣ Preheat the oven to 200°C, and butter 6 ramekin dishes or dariole moulds.

‣ Gently melt the chocolate in a bowl set over a pan of gently simmering water, making sure the bowl does not come into contact with the water.

‣ Add the sugar, butter, eggs and vanilla essence to the bowl and attach the K beater. Mix on a medium speed until pale and fluffy.

‣ Pour in the melted chocolate and mix well, turn the speed to low and gently fold in the flour.

‣ Pour the mixture into the moulds and **cook for about 12 minutes,** until they have a soft spring to them.

‣ Leave to cool for 5 minutes and serve with the ice cream.

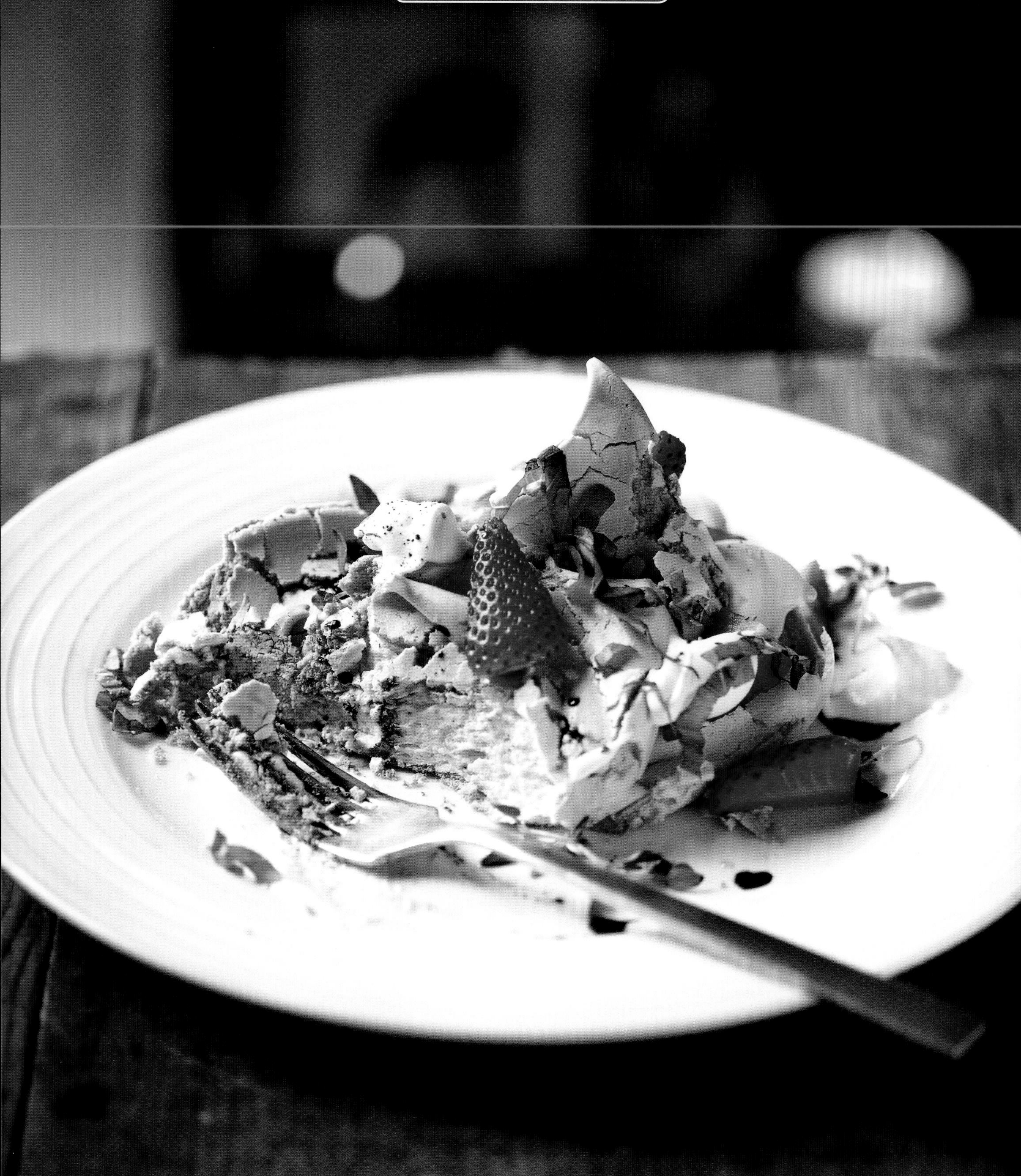

BALSAMIC, THYME AND PEPPER MERINGUES WITH BASIL STRAWBERRIES

SERVES	4
PREP TIME	10 minutes
COOKING TIME	40 minutes plus cooling
TEMPERATURE	150°C / Gas 2
DIFFICULTY	◔ ◔
EQUIPMENT	Baking tray, baking paper
TOOLS	

INGREDIENTS

4 egg whites

200g icing sugar

2 tbsp thyme leaves

1 tsp ground black pepper

4 tbsp balsamic vinegar

1 punnet of strawberries, hulled and quartered

4 tbsp basil leaves, shredded

Cream, to serve

METHOD

➤ Preheat the oven to 150°C and line a baking tray with baking paper.

➤ Attach the whisk, add the egg whites, whisk on a medium speed until you have stiff peaks.

➤ Add the icing sugar one tablespoon at a time until the mix is glossy.

➤ Loosely stir in the thyme, pepper and balsamic vinegar.

➤ Spoon the meringue mixture onto the lined baking tray into fist sized portions, leaving a large gap between each. Drizzle a little balsamic vinegar over each meringue.

➤ **Cook in the oven for 35-40 minutes.** Turn the oven off and leave to cool in the oven.

➤ Serve with the strawberries, shredded basil leaves and a good spoonful of cream.

CHEF'S TIP

The vinegar in this, as well as complementing the strawberries, makes the meringues crisp on the outside and deliciously chewy within.

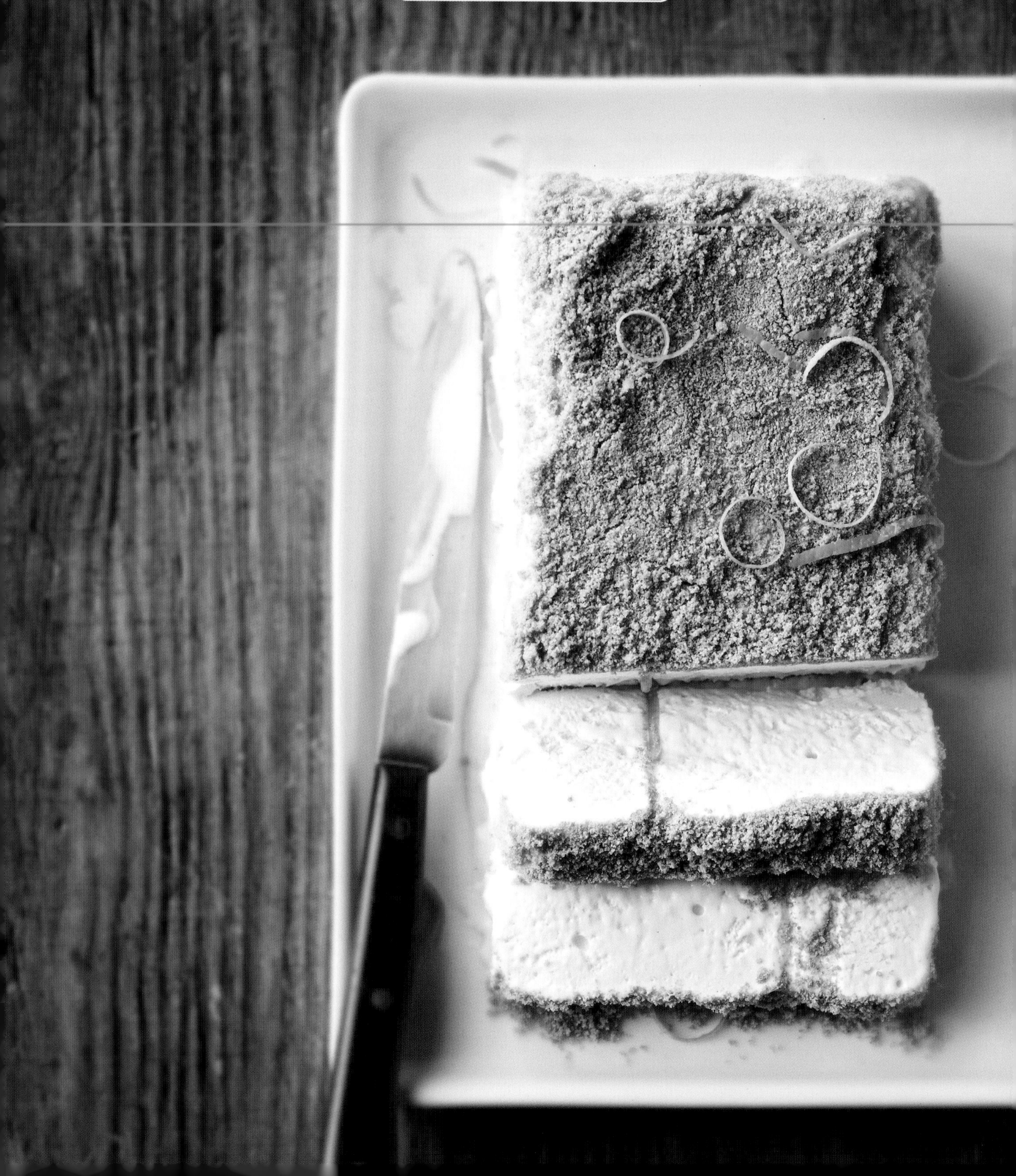

GINGER AND LEMON PARFAIT WITH GINGER BISCUIT CRUMBS

SERVES	6-8
PREP TIME	10 minutes, plus at least 6 hours freezing time (overnight would be better)
DIFFICULTY	✪
EQUIPMENT	900g loaf tin
TOOLS	

INGREDIENTS

30g butter, softened for greasing

12 ginger biscuits

2 eggs

1 tbsp ground ginger

2 tbsp ginger wine

Zest and juice of 1 lemon

180g caster sugar

500ml double cream

METHOD

▸ Grease and line a 900g loaf tin with clear film, grease the inside of the clear film as well.

▸ Attach the food processor with the knife blade, add the ginger biscuits and mix until you have crumbs.

▸ Pour in nearly all of the biscuit crumbs into the loaf tin, reserving some for the end.

▸ Attach the whisk and whisk together the eggs, ground ginger, ginger wine, lemon juice, zest, and sugar until light and creamy. Pour into a separate bowl and reserve.

▸ With the whisk still attached whip the cream until soft peaks form. Remove the whisk and add the creaming beater or folding tool.

▸ Gently fold in the reserved egg mixture on a low speed. Pour into the prepared tin. Cover with clear film and freeze overnight, or for at least six hours.

▸ Turn out of the tin and sprinkle on the remaining crushed biscuits - serve.

CREMA CATALAN WITH EARL GREY SPONGES

THIS CATALAN VERSION OF THE CRÈME BRÛLÉE GOES WELL WITH THE BERGAMOT FLAVOURED EARL GREY SPONGES.

SERVES	4
PREP TIME	15 minutes, plus overnight for chilling
COOKING TIME	60 minutes plus chilling
TEMPERATURE	150°C / Gas 2
DIFFICULTY	◉ ◉
EQUIPMENT	4 crème brulée dishes, deep sided baking tray, baking tray, baking paper
TOOLS	

INGREDIENTS

For the Crema Catalan:

400ml milk
Zest of 1 lemon and 1 orange
1 cinnamon stick
1 tbsp sherry
4 egg yolks
65g caster sugar
1 tbsp vanilla extract
140ml double cream
2 tbsp Demerera sugar

For the Earl Grey sponges:

100g caster sugar
2 eggs
100g butter, melted
100g self raising flour
Leaves from an Earl Grey teabag

METHOD

➤ *To make the Crema Catalan:* preheat the oven to 150°C.

➤ Add the milk, lemon zest, orange zest and cinnamon stick to a pan, bring to just below the boil. Pour in the sherry, turn off and leave to infuse for 15-30 minutes.

➤ Add the egg yolks, sugar and vanilla extract to the bowl. Attach the whisk and whisk on a medium speed until frothy and pale.

➤ Remove the whisk and attach the blender. Add the mixture and the cream to the blender and blend until smooth.

➤ Pour immediately into the four crème brulée dishes and place into the deep sided baking tray half filled with hot water. **Bake in the oven for 65 minutes,** until just set. Remove from the oven and chill in the fridge, preferably overnight, but for at least 2 hours.

➤ *To make the Earl Grey sponges:* Preheat the oven to 190°C and line a baking tray with greaseproof paper.

➤ Add the sugar and eggs to the bowl, attach the whisk and whisk until light and fluffy. Remove the whisk and attach the K beater add half the butter and half the flour and slowly mix.

➤ Add the remaining flour and butter along with the tea leaves and mix on a slow speed until combined.

➤ Spoon tablespoons of the mixture onto the lined baking tray, making sure you leave space between each one. **Bake in the oven for 10 minutes,** or until turning golden. Leave to cool on a wire rack, dust with icing sugar.

➤ Remove the Crema Catalans from the fridge and sprinkle each with a tablespoon of demerera sugar. Caramelise the sugar under a very hot grill. Serve with the sponges and a cup of Earl Grey tea.

CHEF'S TIP

....

Try using Lapsang Suchong for a smokier sponge. Or even add jasmine leaves and candied orange zest.

....

LIMONCELLO AND LEMON TART WITH LAVENDER

SERVES	6-8
PREP TIME	30 minutes plus 1/2 hour chilling
COOKING TIME	50 minutes
TEMPERATURE	200°C / Gas 6
DIFFICULTY	☺ ☺
EQUIPMENT	20cm tart tin, baking paper, baking beans
TOOLS	

INGREDIENTS

For the base:

250g plain flour
125g unsalted butter
125g sugar
1 egg
Zest of 1 lemon
1 tsp lavender flowers

For the filling:

5 eggs
180g caster sugar
Juice and zest of 5 lemons
180ml double cream
20ml Limoncello
Lavender leaves

METHOD

▸ Preheat the oven to 200°C and grease a 20cm tart case.

▸ *For the base:* add the flour, butter, sugar, egg, lemon zest and lavender to the bowl, attach the dough hook and knead on a medium speed until it comes together as a dough. Remove from the bowl, flatten slightly and cover with clear film. Chill in the fridge for half an hour.

▸ Remove the pastry from the fridge and roll out onto a lightly floured surface to a 5mm thick circle, place it into the tart tin making sure it covers the edges. Lay greaseproof paper over the pastry and fill with baking beans or rice and **bake in the oven for 10 minutes.**

▸ Turn the oven to 180°C, remove the beans, trim the pastry from the edges (if necessary) and **bake for a further 10 minutes.** Remove from the oven and leave to cool.

▸ *For the filling:* attach the whisk and whisk the eggs and sugar on a low speed. Add the lemon juice, zest, cream and Limoncello and whisk until combined.

▸ Pour the mixture into the tart case and bake for about half an hour, or until it is lightly set.

▸ Remove from the oven and dust with sugar and lavender leaves.

▸ Leave to cool then serve at room temperature or chill for up to 2 days.

ROAST PEACHES WITH WHITE WINE, PEPPER AND STAR ANISE

SERVES	4
PREP TIME	5 minutes
COOKING TIME	25 minutes
TEMPERATURE	200°C / Gas 6
DIFFICULTY	☻
EQUIPMENT	Oven proof dish, saucepan
TOOLS	

INGREDIENTS

6 peaches, ever so slightly under ripe
12 peppercorns
2 star anise
A pinch of salt
1 vanilla pod, split down the middle
100g caster sugar
50ml water
100ml cream
125ml white wine
Olive oil
Cream to serve

METHOD

▶ Preheat the oven to 200°C.

▶ Halve the peaches and remove the stones then evenly place the fruit skin side down in an oven proof dish.

▶ Attach the compact chopper/grinder with the peppercorns and star anise. Grind on a medium speed until powdered, reserve.

▶ Put the vanilla pod, sugar and water in a saucepan and gently bring to the boil. Stir and cook for a further five minutes until you have a syrup. Add the powdered spices and stir well, reserve.

▶ Remove the vanilla pod and pour a little of the syrup over each peach. **Cook in the oven for 25 minutes,** or until the peaches are soft but still holding their shape. Remove from the oven and leave to cool for a few minutes.

▶ Boil the white wine in a saucepan for a couple of minutes.

▶ Attach the whisk pour in the cream and whisk on a high speed until soft peaks form, reserve.

▶ Remove the whisk and attach the K beater. Put four of the peach halves in the bowl. Turn the machine to a medium speed and slowly add the olive oil, turn up the speed to high and pour in the boiled white wine, mix well to form a puree.

▶ Serve the peach halves with the purée, syrup and whipped cream.

CHEF'S TIP

....

Try apricots, pears or even watermelon to change things around a little. The spices will complement them beautifully.

....

ATTACHMENTS

KENWOOD KITCHEN MACHINES ARE ROBUST, POWERFUL AND FULLY VERSATILE.

They have power outlets where you can attach additional attachments for all your preparation needs including; blending, slicing, grating, chopping, grinding, juicing and much more!

This chapter is a guide to all the additional attachments that are available with recipe suggestions to match. You can also integrate the attachments within the other recipes in the book to help with all of your preparation needs.

SLICING, GRATING AND DICING

KENWOOD'S FOOD PREPARATION ATTACHMENTS ARE IDEAL FOR SLICING, GRATING, JULIENNE/CHIPPING, CHOPPING AND DICING. ALL OF THE ATTACHMENTS WITHIN THIS GROUP HAVE THEIR OWN EXPERTISE AND CAN OFFER A VARIETY OF HELP ON ALL PREPARATION NEEDS.

WHEN BEST TO USE:

VEGETABLE PREPARATION/FRUIT
Slice/grate/julienne or dice a variety of hard and soft vegetables e.g. salads.

CHEESE
Slice/grate/rasping or dice different cheeses for a variety of dishes e.g. cheese souffle.

CHOCOLATE AND NUTS
Grate or rasping chocolate for a variety of dishes e.g. cakes.

FOR MORE INFORMATION VISIT
KENWOODWORLD.COM

FOOD PROCESSOR
Slice or grate ingredients straight into the bowl with **6 stainless steel discs**; thin slice, thick slice, thin grate, thick grate, extra fine grating and julienne. **Stainless steel knife blade is also included** which is ideal for chopping ingredients to make dips and sauces.

CONTINUOUS SLICER/GRATER
Slice or grate continuously on a high speed, ideal for batch cooking and large quantities of ingredients. **Includes 7 stainless steel discs**; thin slicing, thick slicing, thin grating, thick grating, extra fine grating, fine julienne and thick julienne.

ROTARY SLICER/GRATER
Slice or grate on a slow speed, ideal for chocolate, cheese and nuts which need a slower speed to achieve the best result. **Includes 5 drums** for thin slicing, thick slicing, thin grating, thick grating and extra fine grating.

DICING ATTACHMENT
Dice a variety of vegetables, fruits, meat and cheeses ideal for salads, stews and side dishes, **includes a stainless steel slicing disc and dicing grid** producing 10mm x 10mm cubes.

POTATO ROSTI

SERVES	4
PREP TIME	10 minutes
COOKING TIME	10 minutes

INGREDIENTS
2 large Maris Piper or King Edward potatoes
1 tbsp cornflour or potato flour
2 tbsp melted butter
Salt and pepper

METHOD
▸ Peel the potatoes

▸ Attach either one of the below to your machine;

- Food processor with thick grating disc

- Continuous slicer/grater with the thick grating disc

- Rotary slicer/grater with the thick grating drum

▸ Grate the potato and set aside in a bowl.

▸ Add the cornflour, butter, salt and pepper and mix well with a wooden spoon.

▸ Shape into flat round discs approximately 8cm in diameter and 2cm tall (the mixture should make 4).

▸ Heat a pan with a little butter and fry gently for about 4 minutes on each side until golden and cooked through.

CHOPPING AND GRINDING

KENWOOD'S CHOPPING AND GRINDING ATTACHMENTS ARE IDEAL FOR CHOPPING AND GRINDING HERBS, NUTS AND COFFEE, GRINDING MEAT AND FISH AND GRINDING GRAINS, PULSES AND RICE. ALL ATTACHMENTS WITHIN THIS GROUP HAVE THEIR OWN EXPERTISE AND CAN OFFER A VARIETY OF HELP ON ALL CHOPPING AND GRINDING NEEDS.

WHEN BEST TO USE:

HERBS/NUTS
Chop herbs and nuts to use within cooking and baking.

COFFEE
Grind coffee beans into a fine powder.

MEAT
Grind a variety of meat to use within different dishes or to make burgers and sausages.

GRAINS/PULSES/RICE
Grind grains and pulses to make homemade flour for baking.

FOR MORE INFORMATION VISIT
KENWOODWORLD.COM

COMPACT CHOPPER/GRINDER

Chop or grind small portions of ingredients, ideal for herbs, coffee beans, baby food, spices and nuts. **Includes 4 storage glass jars with lids** for milling and storage.

MEAT GRINDER

Produce fresh minced meat or fish, ideal for a variety of dishes including burgers, lasagne and fish cakes. **Comes with 3 metal screens** for fine, medium and coarse results, 2 sized sausage adaptors and Kebbe maker for Middle Eastern dishes.

GRINDING MILL

Grind grains and pulses, ideal for making homemade flour to use in baking, also a good way to help control allergies by making gluten free flour.

PORK, RED WINE AND GARLIC SAUSAGE

SERVES	4
PREP TIME	10 minutes, chilling time 12 hours

INGREDIENTS

1kg pork shoulder
500g pork fat, put in the freezer for at least an hour
100ml red wine
3 cloves of garlic, crushed
Leaves from 2 thyme sprigs, finely chopped
200cm sausage skin
1 tbsp salt
A large twist of pepper

METHOD

▸ Attach the food mincer and fit the medium screen.

▸ Cut the pork shoulder into cubes and feed through the mincer. Put in a large bowl, cover and keep in the fridge.

▸ Remove the fat from the freezer and cut into cubes. Feed through the mincer and add to the meat in the fridge.

▸ Take the meat and fat from the fridge and add the red wine, garlic and thyme. Add the salt and pepper and mix really well, reserve in the fridge.

▸ Remove the medium disc and attach the sausage making attachment.

▸ Feed the sausage skin onto the nozzle, and with the machine on slow, feed the meat through the tube. As the skin fills up, twist it every 10cm, depending on how long you like your sausages, laying them on the work surface as they come out.

▸ When you have finished tie the end. Place on a tray and leave to dry for an hour. Place in the fridge overnight.

▸ The sausages are now ready to cook, or you can wrap and save for later. They can be frozen for up to a month.

PASTA ATTACHMENTS

KENWOOD'S PASTA ATTACHMENTS ARE IDEAL FOR CREATING FRESH HOMEMADE PASTA, FROM FLAT SHEETS FOR LASAGNE OR RAVIOLI TO A PASTA SHAPER THAT CAN MAKE UP TO 12 DIFFERENT TYPES OF PASTA INCLUDING FUSILLI AND LINGUINE. PASTA DOUGH CAN BE FLAVOURED WITH HERBS, TOMATO PUREE OR SPINACH TO MAKE A VARIETY OF DIFFERENT PASTA DISHES.

WHEN BEST TO USE:

PASTA DOUGH

Make flat sheets of pasta or a variety of pasta shapes to make the perfect pasta dish.

BREAD/SWEET DOUGH

Rolling out dough so that it can be used to make pies, biscuits etc.

BISCUITS

Make homemade biscuits utilising the biscuit maker attachment.

FOR MORE INFORMATION VISIT **KENWOODWORLD.COM**

FLAT PASTA ROLLER

Make fresh flat sheets of pasta and control the thickness you desire using the adjustable dial, ideal for making lasagne, ravioli or cannelloni. **Includes a roller** to help feed the pasta dough through the roller.

Pasta cutters:

- Tagliatelle Cutter
- Taglioni Cutter
- Trenette Cutter
- Spaghetti Cutter

PASTA SHAPER

Make fresh pasta shapes for a variety of dishes. Thin pastas should be served with thin sauces, while thicker sauces work better with thicker heavier pastas.

12 OPTIONAL DIES AVAILABLE

- Bigoli
- Casarecce
- Maccheroni lisci
- Spaccatelli
- Spaghetti quadri
- Pappardelle
- Silatelli
- Linguine
- Fusilli
- Cochigliette
- Bucatini
- Orecchiette

SPINACH FUSILLI

SERVES	4
PREP TIME	20 minutes
COOKING TIME	3 minutes

INGREDIENTS

For the pasta dough:

500g strong type '00' flour
4 eggs beaten
2 tbsp water (if necessary)
Salt to season
1 tsp dried basil
1 tsp dried oregano
1 tsp dried thyme
200g baby leaf spinach
50g flour

METHOD

- Add the flour and salt to the bowl and attach the dough hook. With the machine running slowly add the eggs and water, gradually increasing the speed until a dough is formed.

- Add the basil, oregano and thyme to the bowl and knead on a medium speed for 5 minutes.

- Remove the dough from the bowl and wrap in clear film. Leave to rest in the fridge for at least half an hour before using.

- Cook the spinach in boiling water for ten seconds then remove and drain in a colander. Leave to cool and squeeze out as much of the excess water as possible, finely chop and reserve.

- Remove the pre-made pasta dough from the fridge and add the chopped spinach, add some more flour if it is becoming too moist.

- Cut the dough into eight and attach the past shaper with the fusilli disc.

- On a low speed feed the dough through the pasta shaper and slice the pasta off after every 4cm until all the dough is used.

- Toss in a little flour and leave to dry for half an hour before cooking.

- Alternatively, dry completely and store in an airtight jar for up to a month.

JUICING

KENWOOD'S JUICING ATTACHMENTS ARE IDEAL FOR CREATING FRESH FRUIT OR VEGETABLE JUICE.

ALL ATTACHMENTS WITHIN THIS GROUP HAVE THEIR OWN EXPERTISE AND CAN OFFER A VARIETY OF JUICE OPTIONS FROM HEALTH DRINKS TO PUREE.

- -

WHEN BEST TO USE:

DRINKS
Juice fruit or vegetables to create fresh fruit juice.

CITRUS JUICE
Squeeze citrus fruits to create fresh fruit juice.

COULIS
Press berries to make coulis to serve with desserts.

TOMATO JUICE
Press tomatoes to make fresh tomato juice to use within a variety of dishes.

 FOR MORE INFORMATION VISIT **KENWOODWORLD.COM**

CITRUS JUICER

Juice citrus fruits straight into the bowl to create fresh fruit juice; ideal for oranges, lemons, limes and grapefruits.

METAL JUICE EXTRACTOR

High speed juicer that enables the user to extract juice quickly and efficiently from whole fruit and vegetables to create a variety of fruit juices, health drinks and smoothies. **Juice jug included** with integrated foam filter to serve only clear fruit juice.

FRUIT PRESS

The slow rotary action of this fruit press enables the end user to extract juice from berries or tomatoes to create healthy juices, and purees or sauces from the removed pulp.

CARROT, BEETROOT AND PEACH SMOOTHIE

SERVES	4
PREP TIME	5 minutes

INGREDIENTS

4 carrots, peeled
2 raw, cleaned beetroot
4 peaches
200ml natural yoghurt

METHOD

▶ Attach the juice extractor and feed the carrots, beetroot and peaches through.

▶ Stir in the yoghurt and serve with ice.

BOWL ATTACHMENTS

KENWOOD OFFERS BOWL
ATTACHMENTS FOR ALL
ADDITIONAL PREPARATION
NEEDS INCLUDING A FROZEN
DESSERT MAKER, PUREE AND
SIEVE AND POTATO PEELER.

FOR MORE
INFORMATION VISIT
KENWOODWORLD.COM

FROZEN DESSERT MAKER

Make homemade ice cream, sorbet and frozen yoghurt within the pre-freeze frozen dessert maker bowl. Leave the bowl in the freezer for 24 hours prior to use, attach to the Kitchen Machine and add fruit and cream to produce delicious and fresh ice cream - you can make any flavour.

PUREE AND SIEVE

Gently puree tomatoes and fruit to create preserves, jelly and coulis. **Comes with two sieve options** for fine and coarse results, the sieve can also be used for sifting flour into a cake mixture.

POTATO PEELER

Quickly and effortlessly peel hard root vegetables in the abrasive bowl attachment giving the peeled vegetable texture ready for roasting.

MANGO AND CHILLI SORBET

SERVES	4
PREP TIME	10 minutes, pre-freeze bowl for 24 hours
COOKING TIME	30 minutes

INGREDIENTS

3 mangoes, peeled and stoned
250g caster sugar
1 red chilli, seeds removed and finely sliced
Juice and zest of 1 lime

METHOD

▸ Attach the blender and add the mangoes, sugar, chilli and lime, blend on a medium speed until combined.

▸ Remove the blender attachment and attach the frozen dessert maker bowl.

▸ On a low speed gradually pour the mango mixture into the bowl.

▸ Leave to churn for about half an hour.

▸ This can be eaten immediately or kept in the freezer.

GLOSSARY

BAKING POWDER

A raising agent consisting of Alkali, such as bicarbonate of soda (baking soda) mixed with acid, usually cream of tartar (tartaric acid). These produce carbon dioxide which expands during cooking and makes cakes rise.

BAKING SODA

Another name for Baking Powder.

BLANCHING/BLANCHED

Briefly immersing food such as vegetables, fruit or nuts in water to help remove the skin, e.g. tomatoes, almonds, peaches; or to serve as a first stage of cooking in the preparation of many dishes.

CHARRED

Cooked until blackened in colouring.

CLEAR FILM

A clear flexible film suitable for covering foods during storage and resting.

CREAMING

The method of beating fat and sugar together to obtain a light airy texture and pale colour. Used in cakes and puddings which contain a high proportion of fat. It helps to incorporate air.

CURE/CURING

The method of curing or preserving meat using a brining or pickling solution (water, salt, nitrites). Used as a way of adding additional flavour to a meat.

CUTLETS

A thin slice of meat, usually veal or lamb, cut from the leg or ribs.

DEGLAZE

Deglaze a pan by moistening and then scraping up the browned bits of food that stick to the bottom of the pan. These deglazed browned bits are loaded with flavour. By deglazing the brown bits, you can transform them into a delicious sauce.

EASY ACTION DRIED YEAST

Dried yeast (or active dried yeast) comes in small granules that are first reconstituted with warm water and sugar; and powdered (or 'easy-blend' or 'fast-action') dried yeast which is sold in sachets and just sprinkled straight into a bowl of flour. An essential ingredient for bread making.

FOLDING IN

A delicate method of combining a whisked or creamed mixture with other ingredients by cutting and folding, so that the mix retains its lightness. Used mainly for soufflés, meringues and light cake mixes.

FRENCH TRIMMED

A way that meat is prepared so that the bone is left protruding.

GELATINE

An animal-derived setting agent available as a powder or as leaf gelatine.

GLOSSY

Smooth and shiny consistency.

INFUSE

A process that involves the soaking or seeping of a substance in hot liquid to extract the flavour of the substance being immersed into the liquid/food item.

KNEAD

A gentle firm action used with bread dough, to develop the gluten in the flour.

KNOCK BACK/KNOCK AIR OUT

To knead yeast dough for the second time, to ensure an even texture.

LOAF TIN

Rectangular high-sided tin for baking bread or cakes.

PIPERADE

A typical Basque dish prepared with onion, green peppers and tomatoes sautéed and flavoured with red peppers.

PUREE

Fruits, vegetables, meat or fish which have been blended, sieved or pounded to a smooth textured pulp.

REDUCE

To make a sauce or liquid more concentrated by fast boiling in an uncovered pan.

REMOVE THE FLESH

Removing the meat from the bones.

RISOTTO

An Italian dish of rice, cooked in butter or oil with stock, meat, seafood or vegetables and often Parmesan cheese.

ROUX

A mixture of equal parts fat and flour used for thickening sauces and soups.

SAUTÉ

To cook food in a small quantity of fat which quickly browns the food.

SEARING

Quickly browning meat in a little hot fat.

SCORE

To cut small slits in a cut of meat, allowing the meat to soak up more of the flavours

SEASONING

Adding condiments, usually salt and pepper to a dish to enhance the flavour.

SELF-RAISING FLOUR

Flour to which a raising agent has been added in order to facilitate the rising of cakes. Can be substituted for plain flour and baking powder.

SIMMERING

Cooking food and liquids slowly and steadily over a gentle heat and keeping just below boiling point.

SOFT/STIFF PEAKS

Refers to the beating or whipping of cream or egg whites. Soft peaks will form a peak but will flop over, whilst with a stiff peak there is no movement and you could turn the bowl upside-down without the contents falling out.

STRONG PLAIN FLOUR

A flour with a high protein content and good gluten content, making it perfect for bread.

WHIPPING

Beating air rapidly into a mixture, using a whisk.

ZEST

The oily outer part of the skin of the citrus fruit, without the pith, used for flavouring.

INDEX OF RECIPES

NOTES AND IDEAS